Find over 120 stickers at the back of this book!

Color by Numbers

ARCTURUS

This edition published in 2024 by Arcturus Publishing Limited
26/27 Bickels Yard, 151–153 Bermondsey Street,
London SE1 3HA

Illustrators: Lizzy Doyle and Claire Stamper
Layout: Duck Egg Blue, Chris Bell, Steve Flight, and Lucy Doncaster
Editors: Kait Eaton with Sebastian Rydberg, and JMS Books llp with Sebastian
Rydberg and Susannah Bailey, and Lucy Doncaster
with thanks to Alana Hassett and Jayne Ross
Managing Editor: Joe Harris
Design Manager: Jessica Holliland

ISBN: 978-1-3988-3595-5
CH011942NT
Supplier 29, Date 1023, PI00005191

Printed in China

Let's color!

This book contains 169 color-by-number illustrations for you to complete—from farm animals and unicorns to fairies and dinosaurs. At the bottom of each page, you will find a color key. Follow this guide to bring the awesome pictures to life. There are also more than 120 stickers at the back of the book for you to use to decorate your finished pictures.

Have you ever petted a pony?

Cats and kittens love to play!

What big teeth you have, Tyrannosaurus Rex!

ty-RAN-oh-SORE-us REX

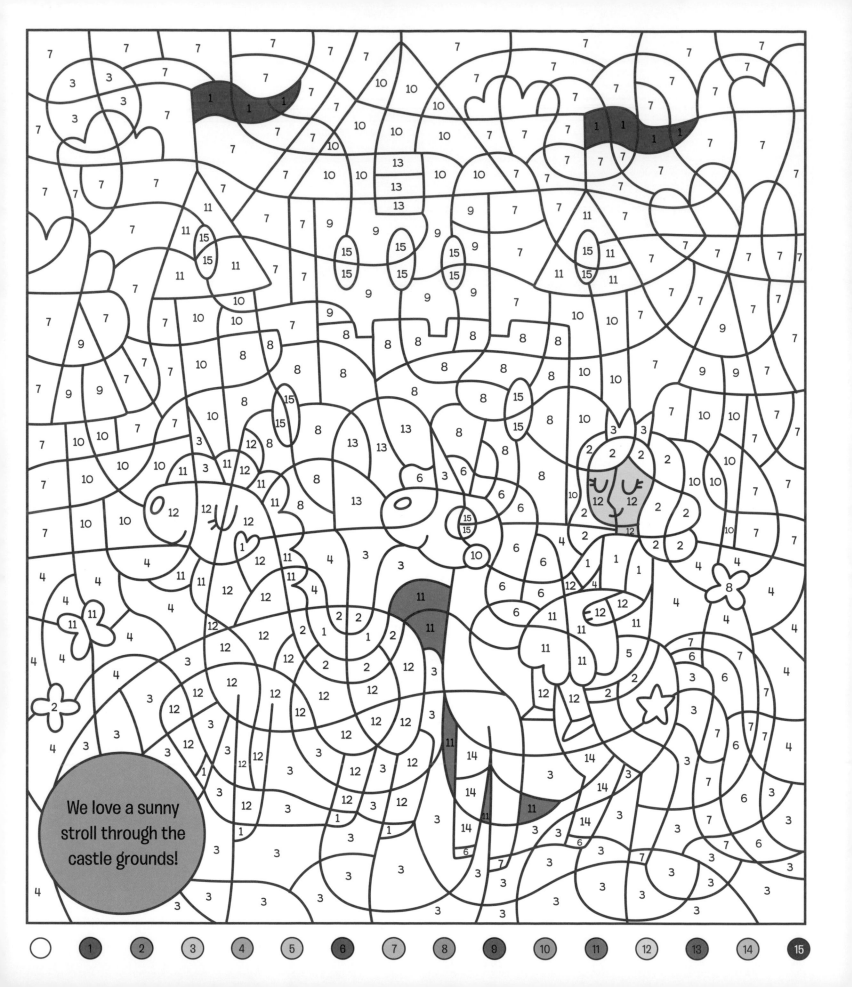

We love a sunny stroll through the castle grounds!

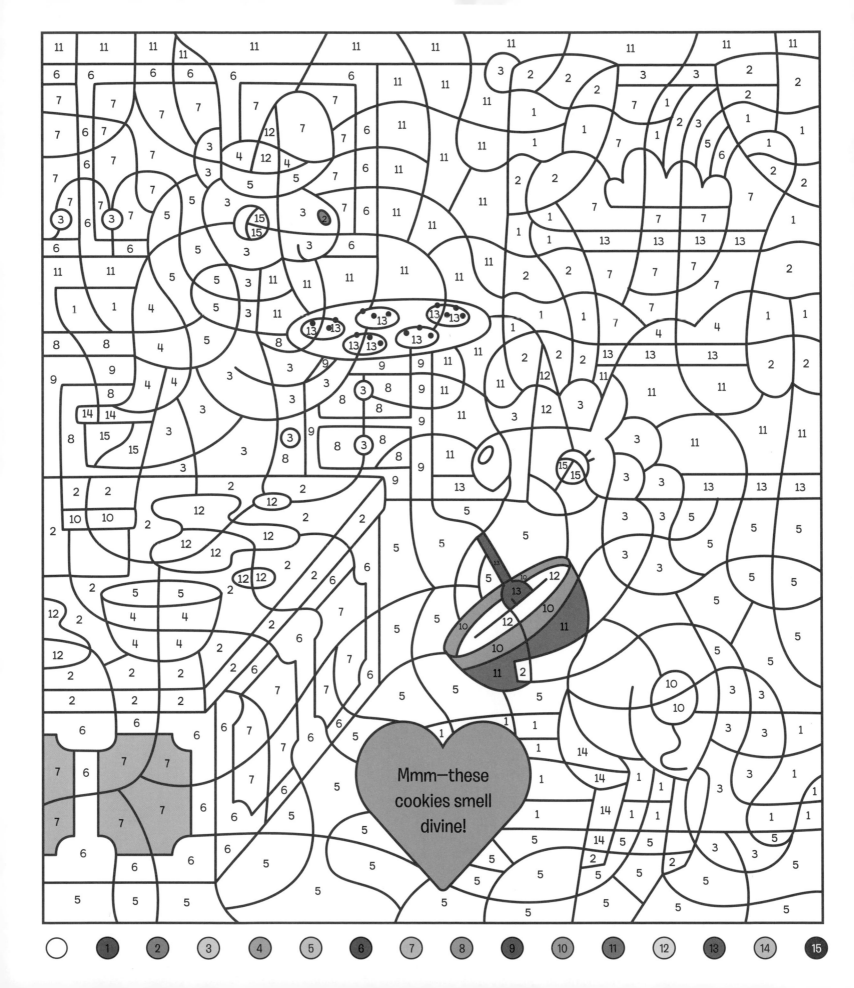

Mmm—these cookies smell divine!

Rabbits often munch on carrots.

The farmer is feeding his chickens.

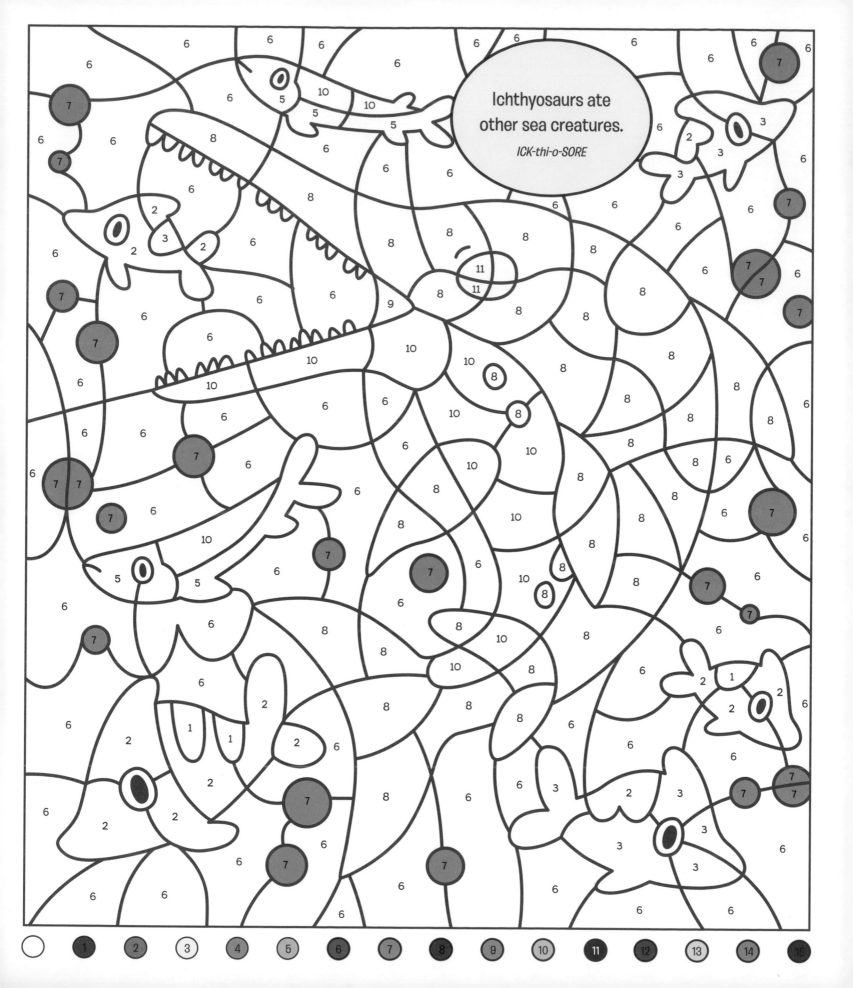

Ichthyosaurs ate other sea creatures.

ICK-thi-o-SORE

Pachycephalosaurus had a thick skull, but a tiny brain.

pak-ee-SEF-ul-lo-SORE-us

The hamster wheel is lots of fun!

The cow and her calf are out in the field.

Pterosaurs flew high in the sky.

TEH-roh-sore

Stegosaurus
had bony plates
along its back.

STEG-oh-SORE-us

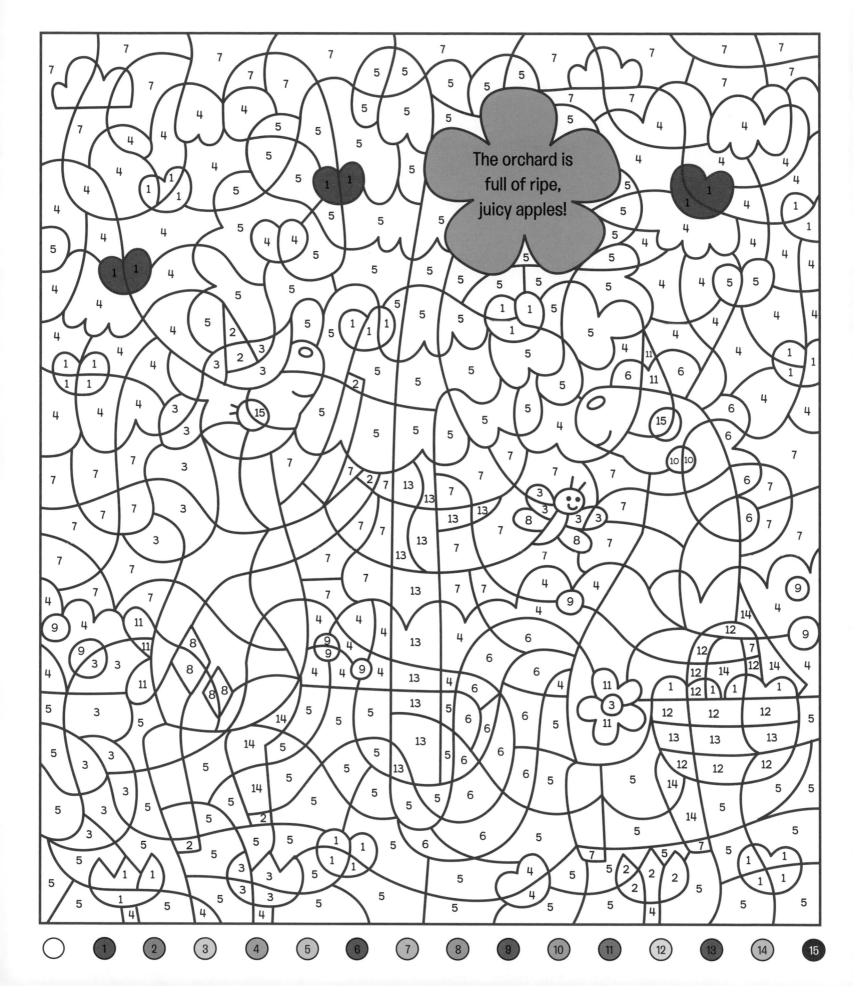

The orchard is full of ripe, juicy apples!

This little girl has a pet snake.

Lambs are usually born in spring.

These Maiasauras have just hatched.

MY-ah-SORE-ah

Dilophosaurus could run very fast.

dy-LOAF-oh-SORE-us

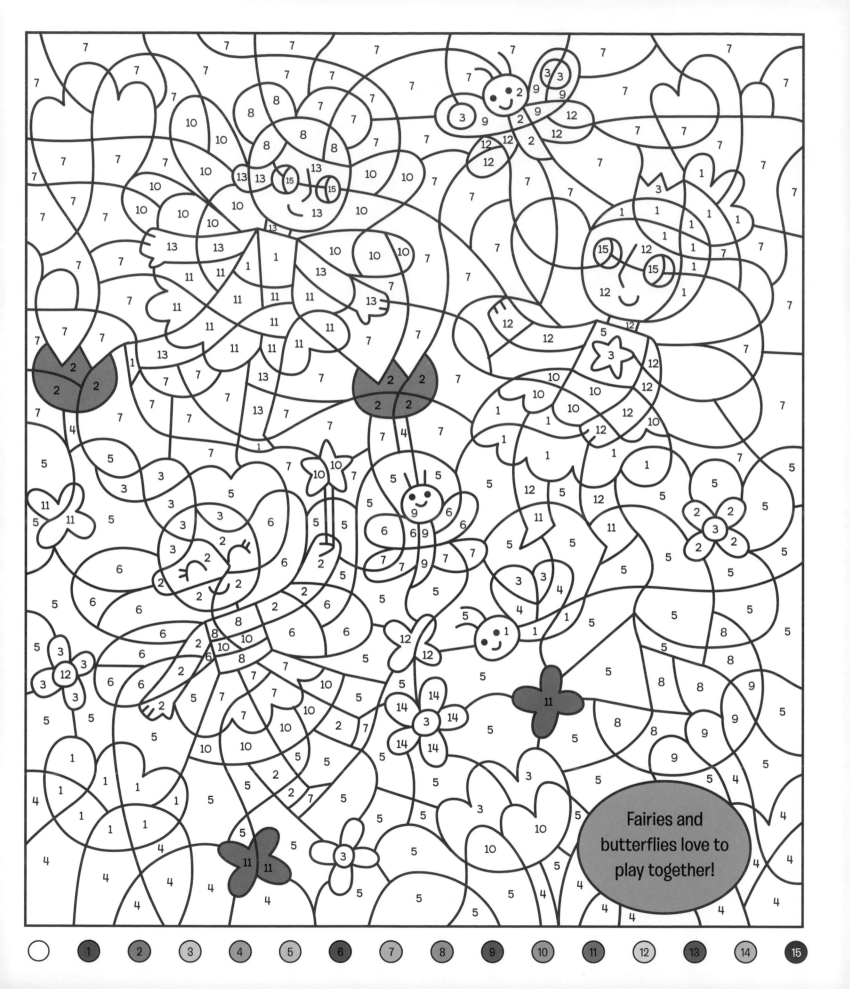

Fairies and butterflies love to play together!

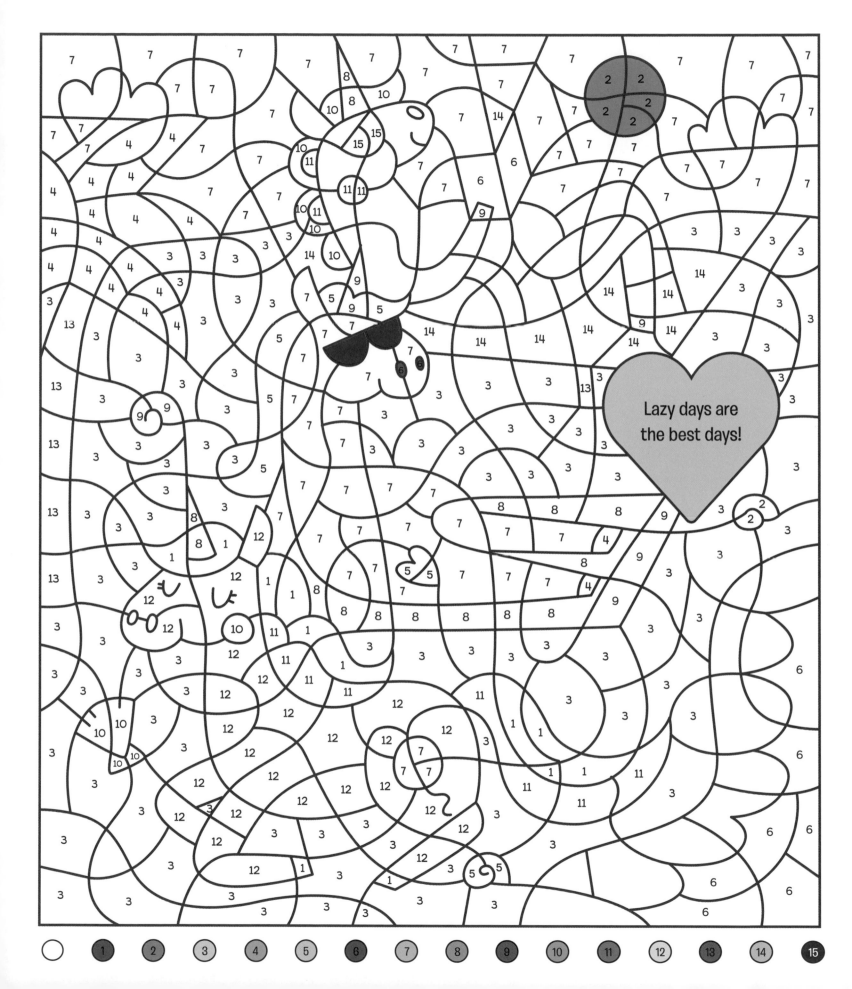

Lazy days are the best days!

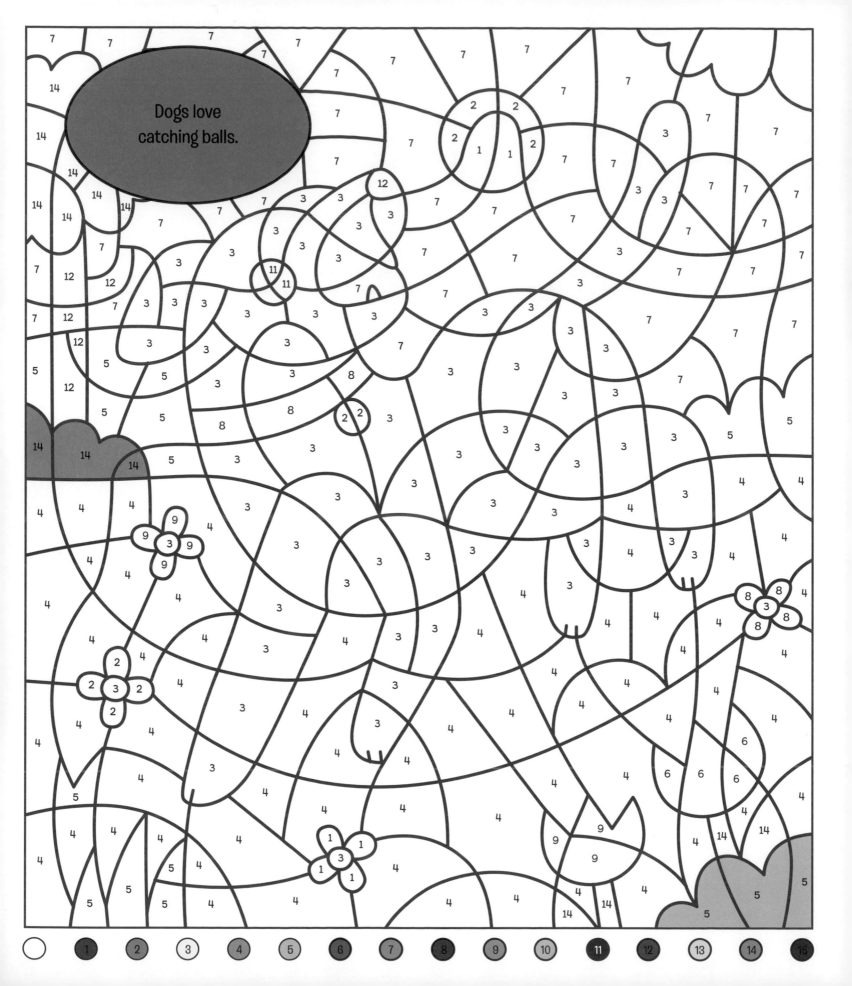

Dogs love catching balls.

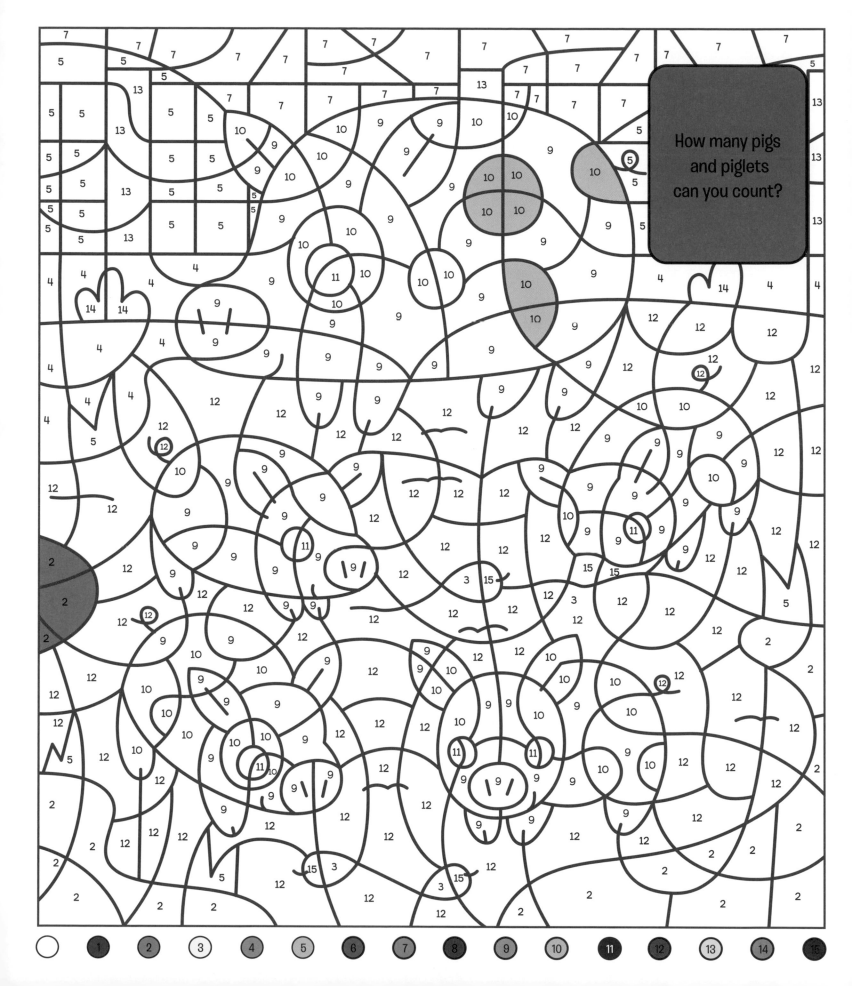

How many pigs
and piglets
can you count?

Triceratops had three horns on its head.

try-SEH-ra-tops

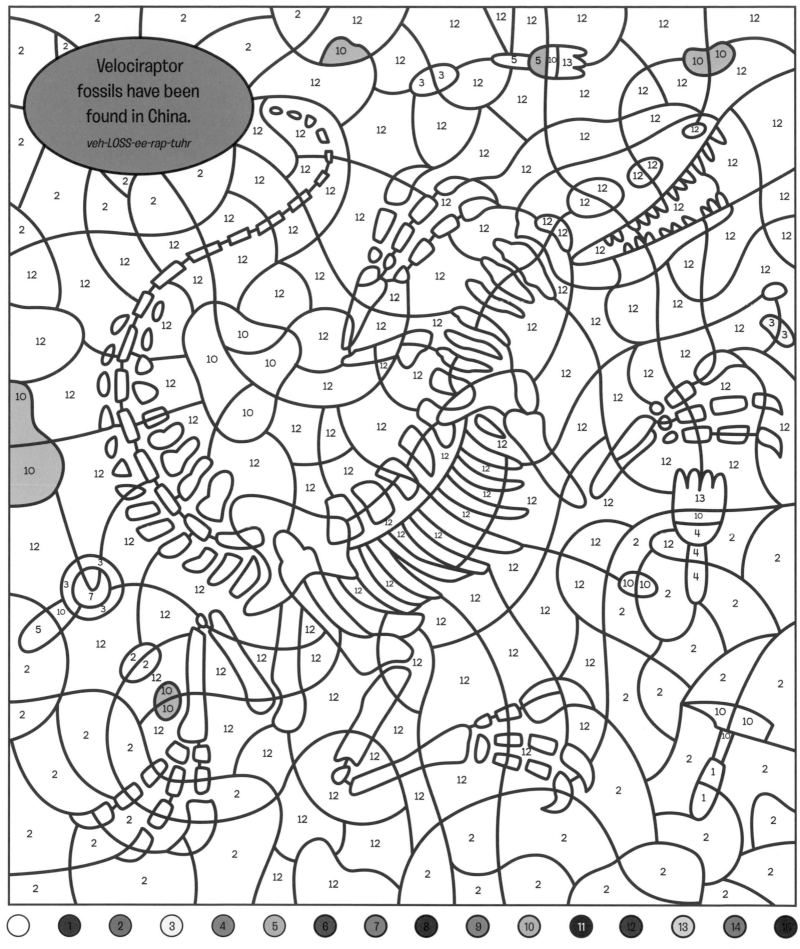

Velociraptor fossils have been found in China.

veh-LOSS-ee-rap-tuhr

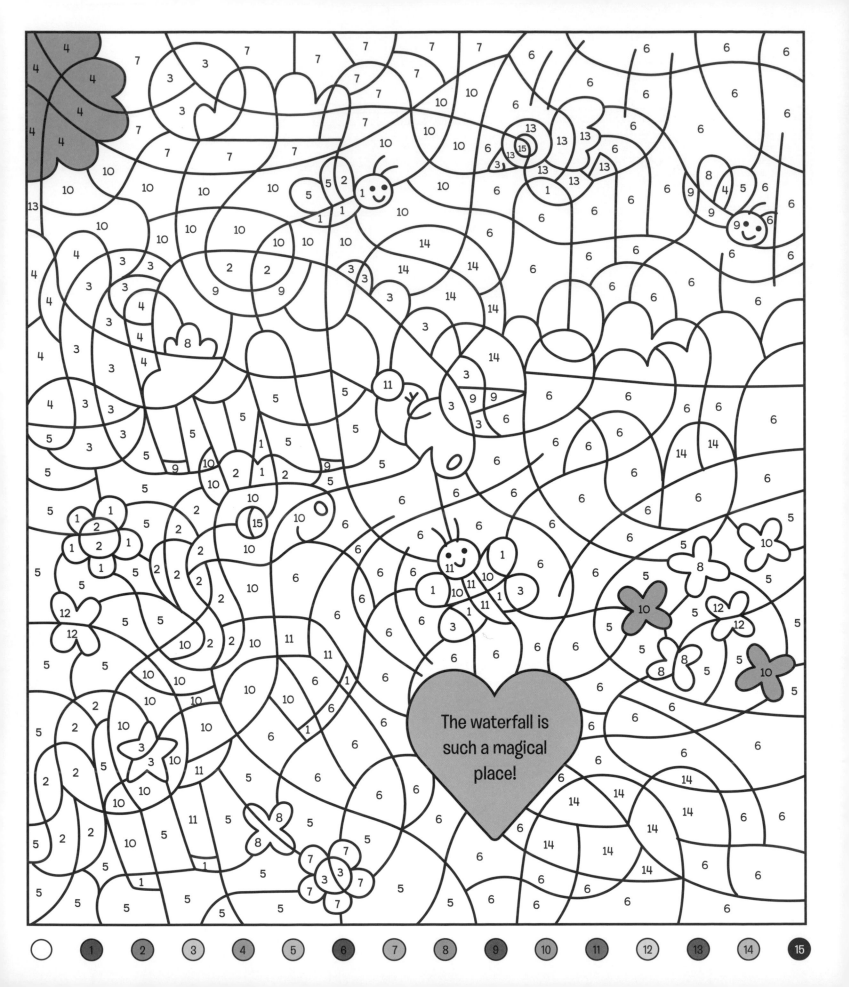

The waterfall is such a magical place!

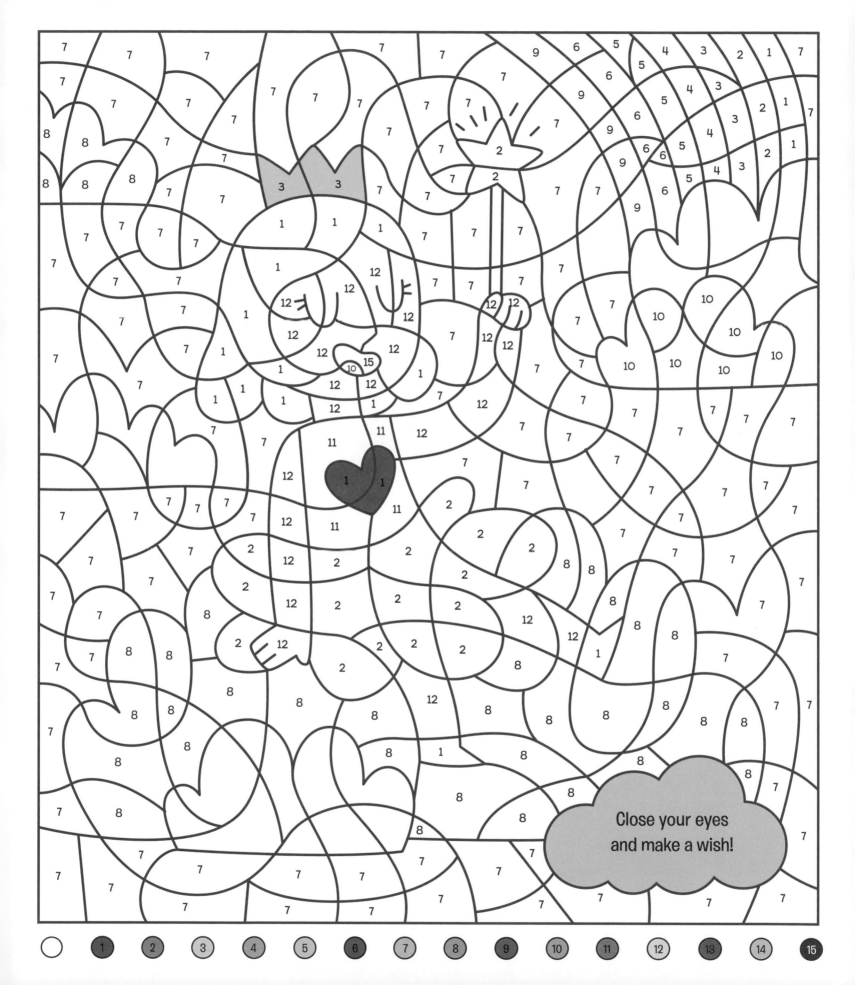

Close your eyes
and make a wish!

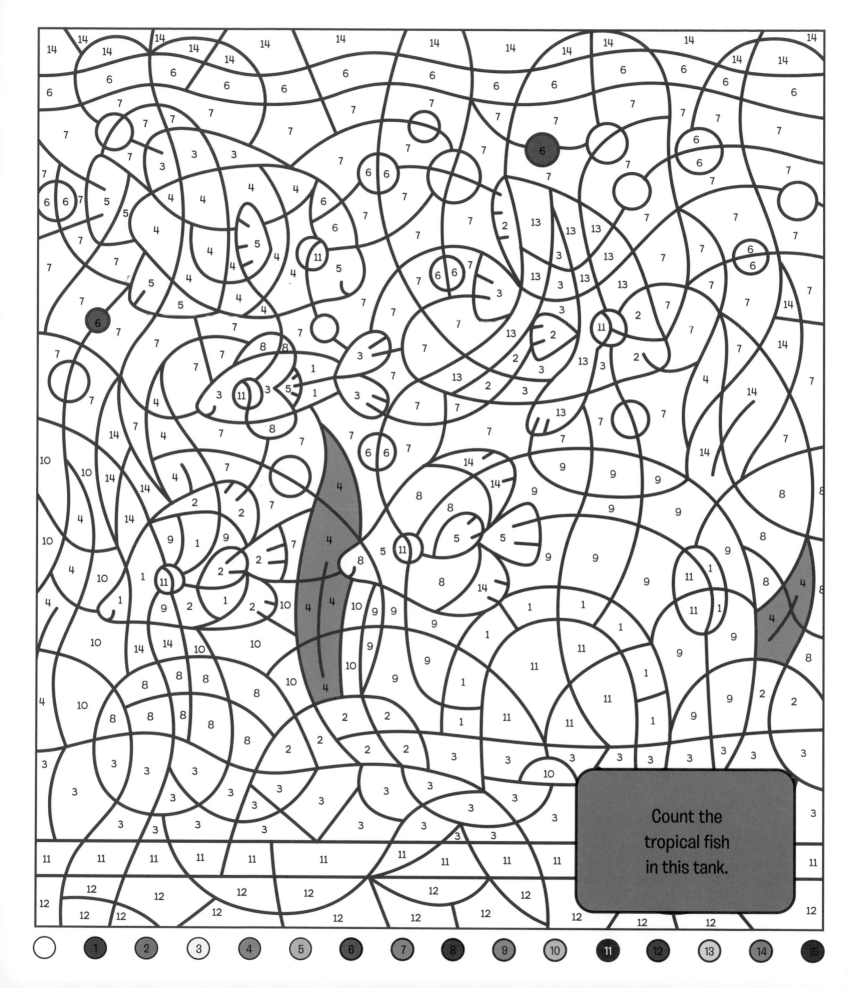

Count the tropical fish in this tank.

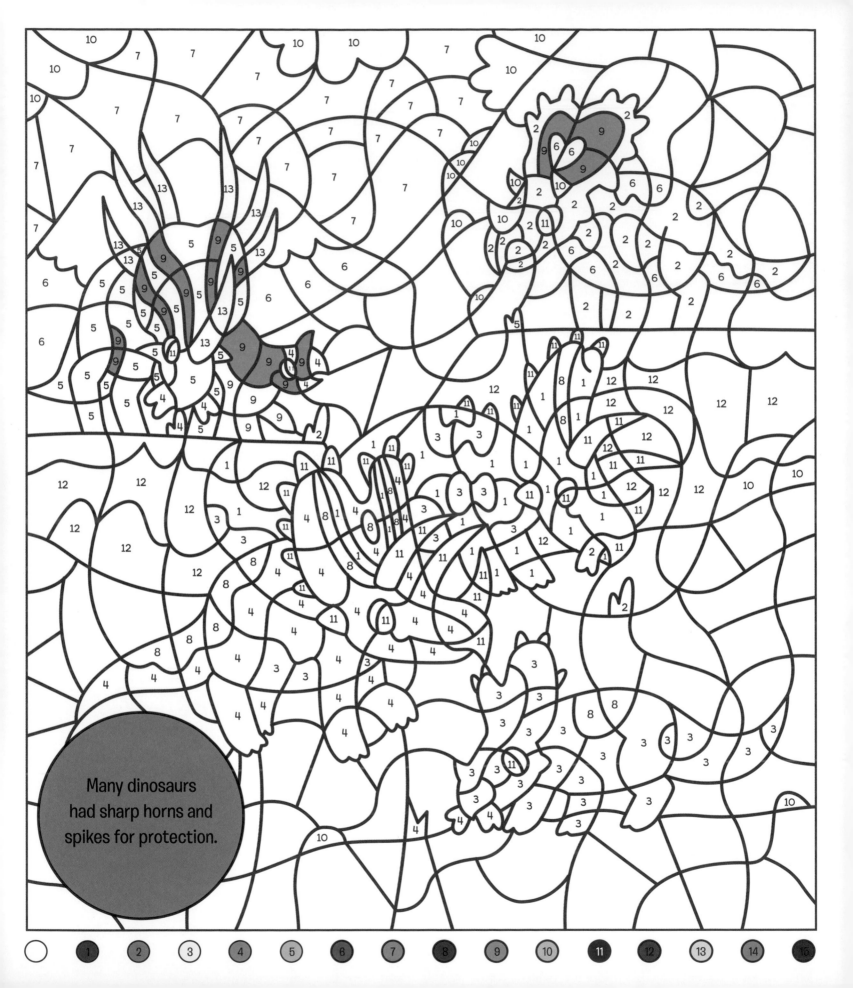

Many dinosaurs had sharp horns and spikes for protection.

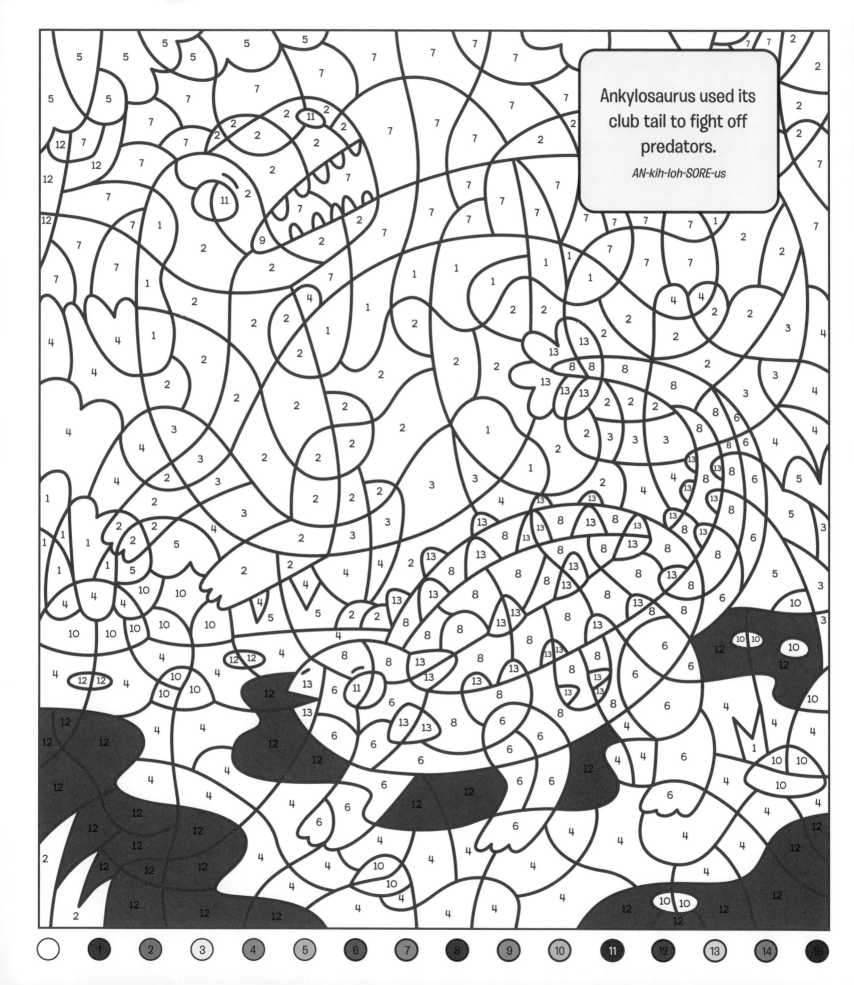

Ankylosaurus used its club tail to fight off predators.

AN-kih-loh-SORE-us

What an enchanting place for a spot of tea!

Baby goats are called "kids."

Turtles sleep all winter.

Archaeopteryx had feathers like a bird!

ARK-ee-OPT-er-ix

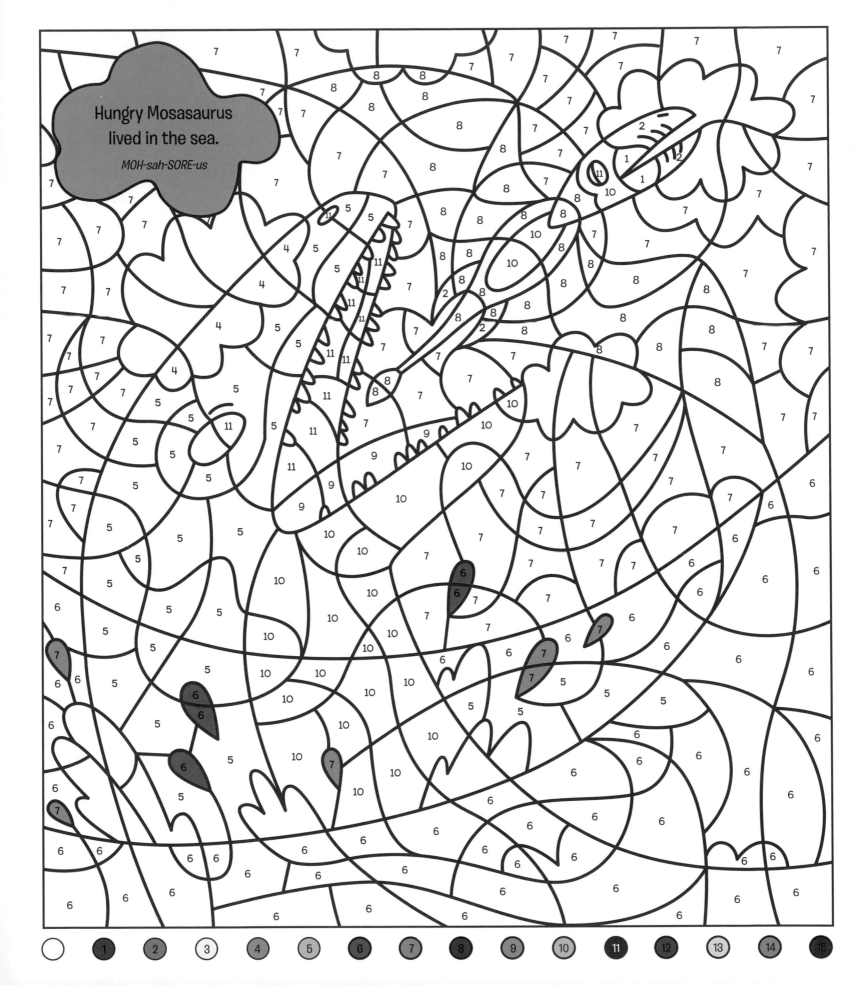

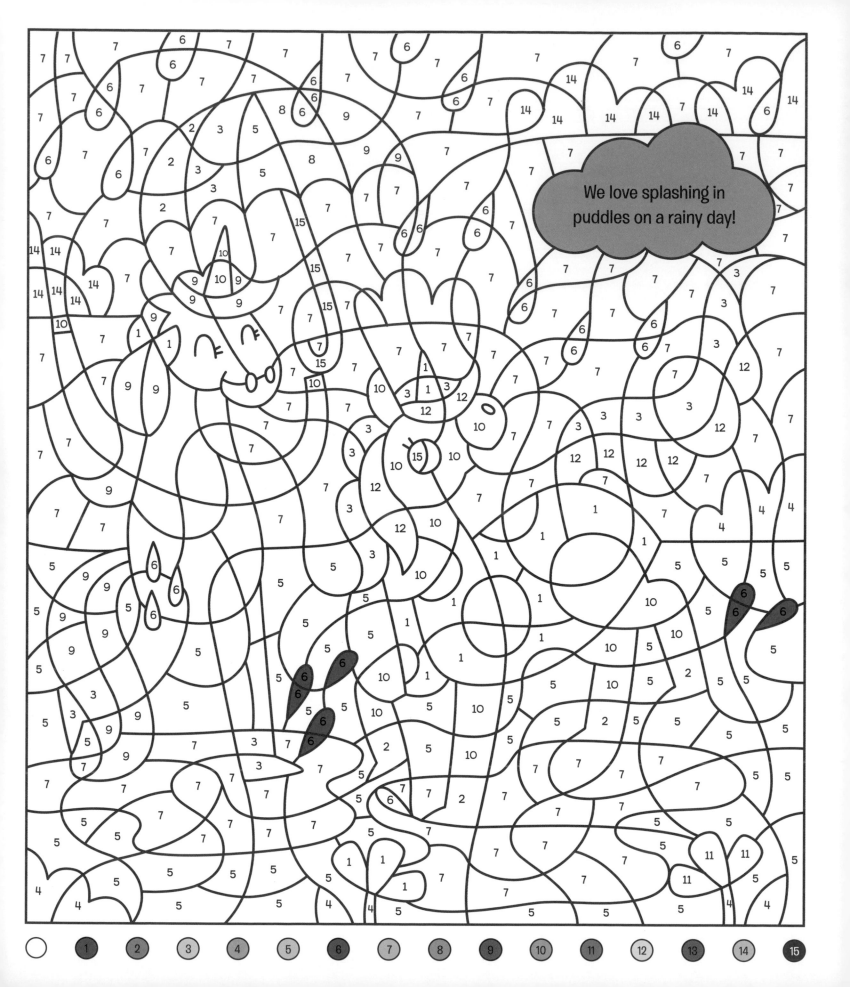

We love splashing in puddles on a rainy day!

So many dazzling jewels to admire!

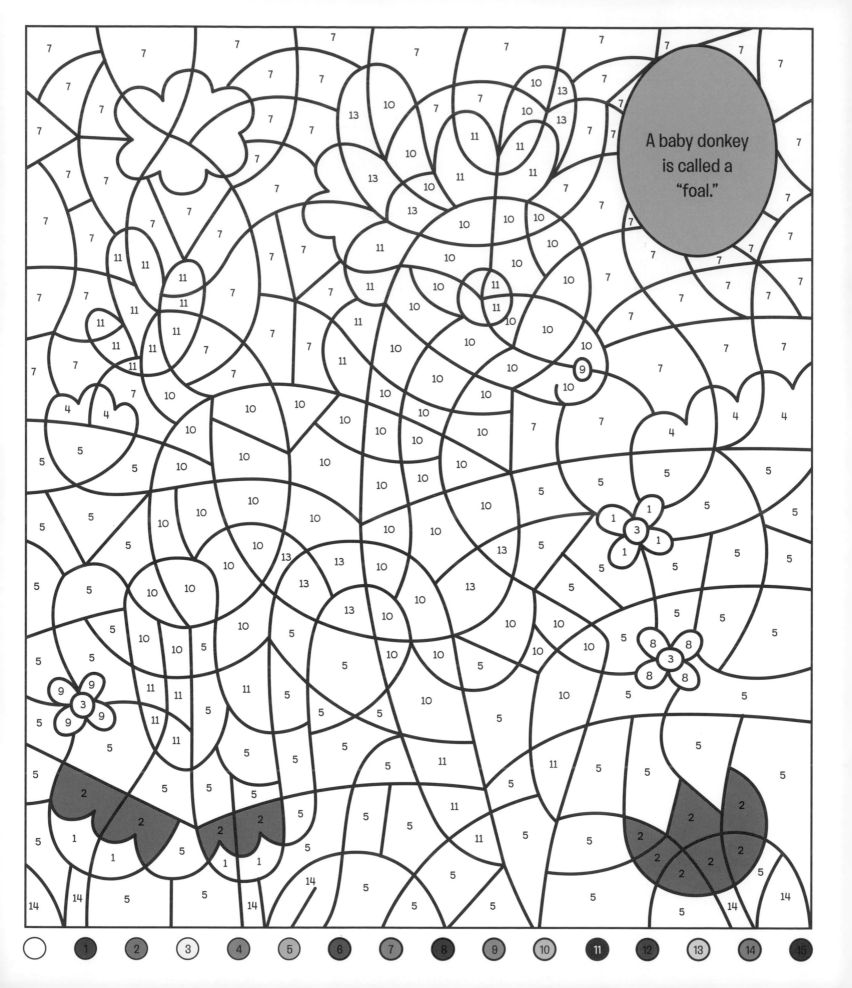

A baby donkey is called a "foal."

These parrots are known as "lovebirds."

Plateosaurus means "flat lizard."

PLAT-ee-o-SORE-us

Raaaar! Who's afraid of Utahraptor?

YOO-tah-RAP-tor

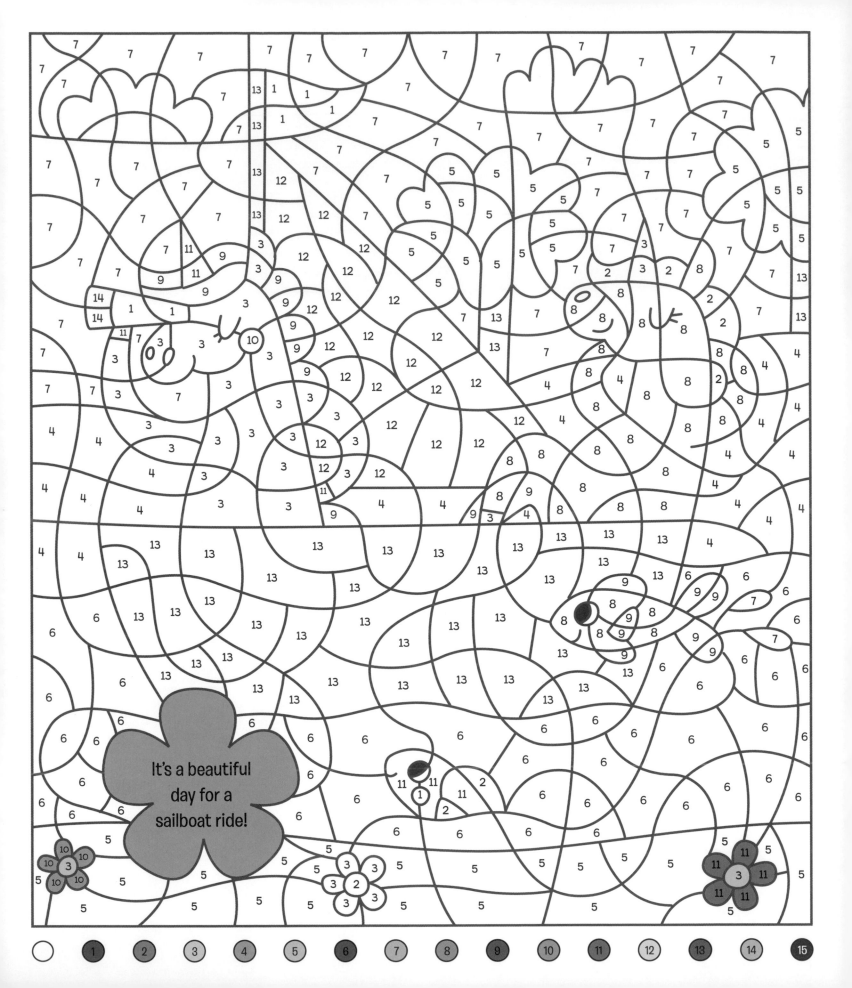

It's a beautiful day for a sailboat ride!

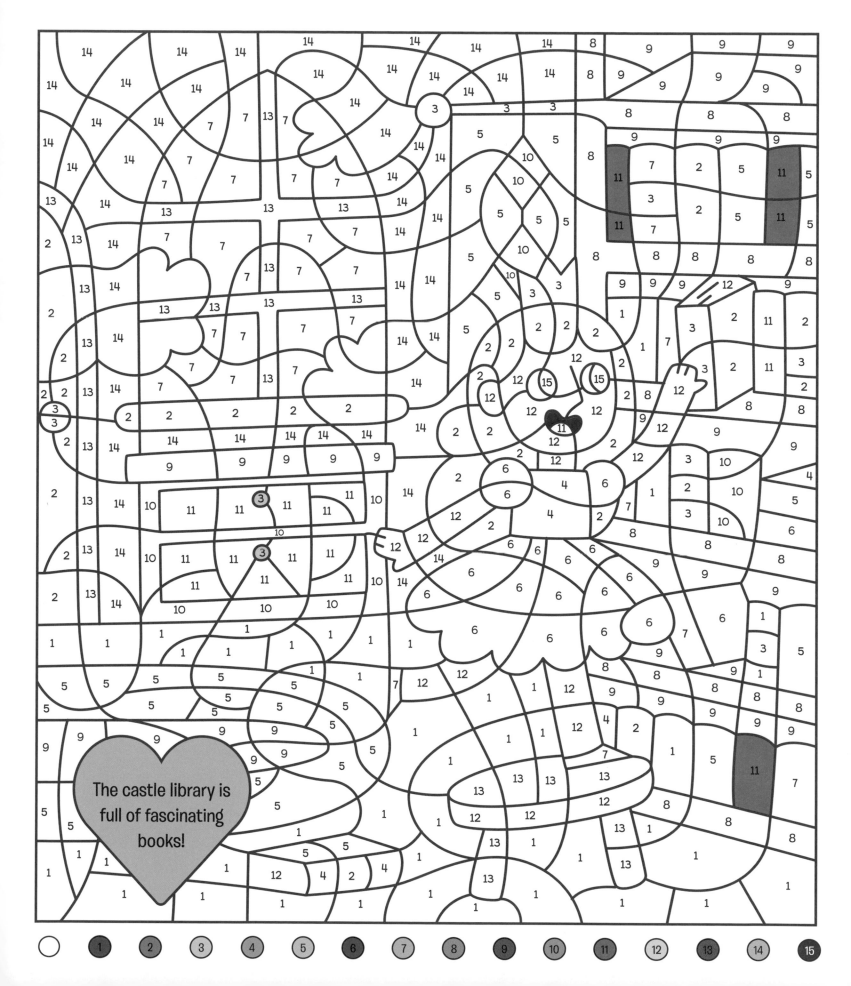

The castle library is full of fascinating books!

Llamas come from South America.

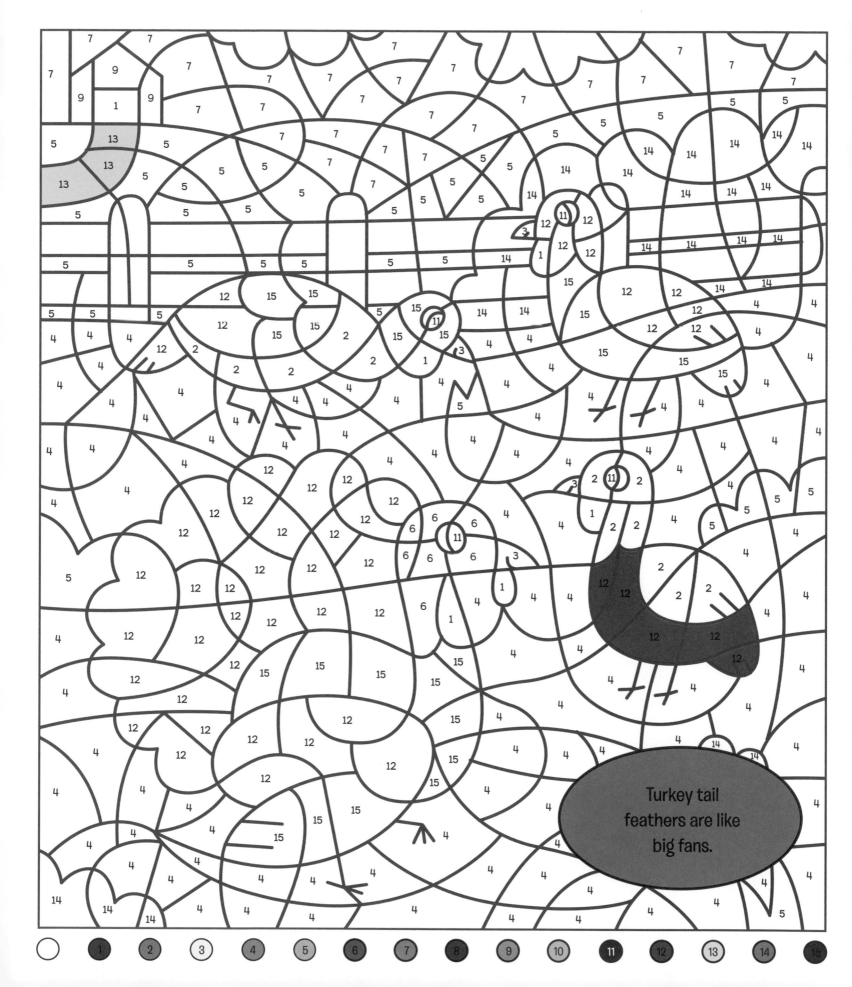

Turkey tail feathers are like big fans.

Dinosaur skeletons are on show at some museums.

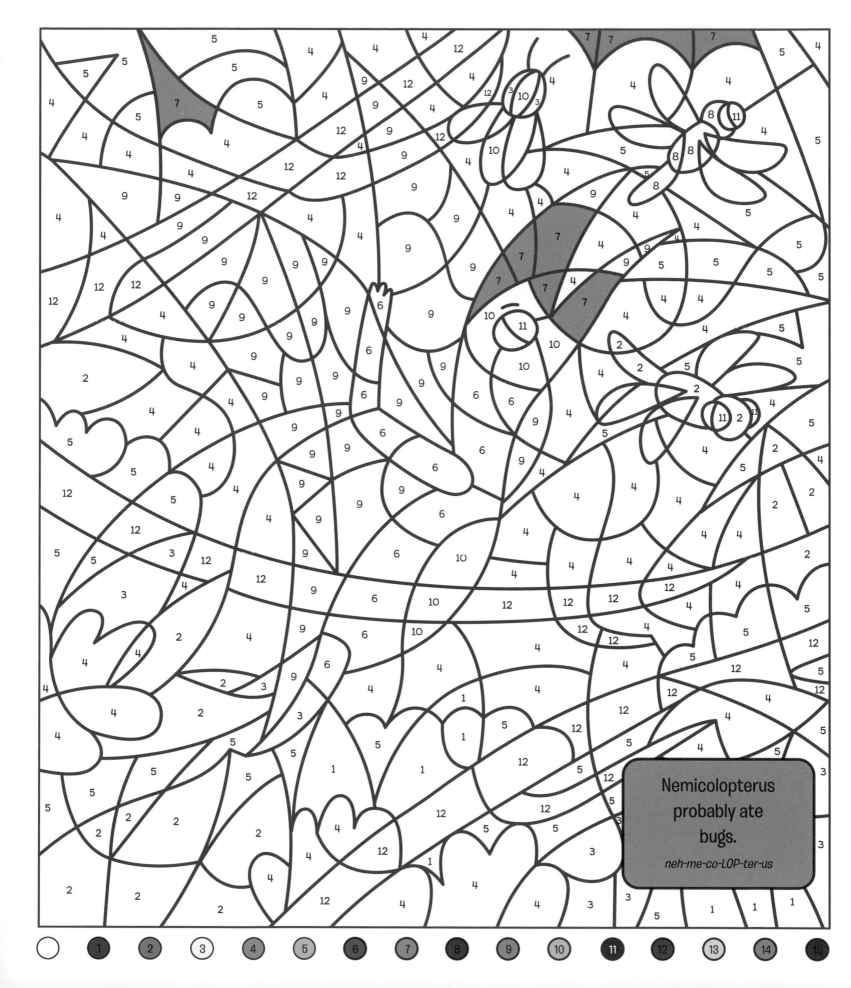

Nemicolopterus
probably ate
bugs.

neh-me-co-LOP-ter-us

Who will win the sandcastle competition?

Oh dear! Watch out for the bumblebee!

Clownfish can live for ten years!

Ostriches are birds that cannot fly.

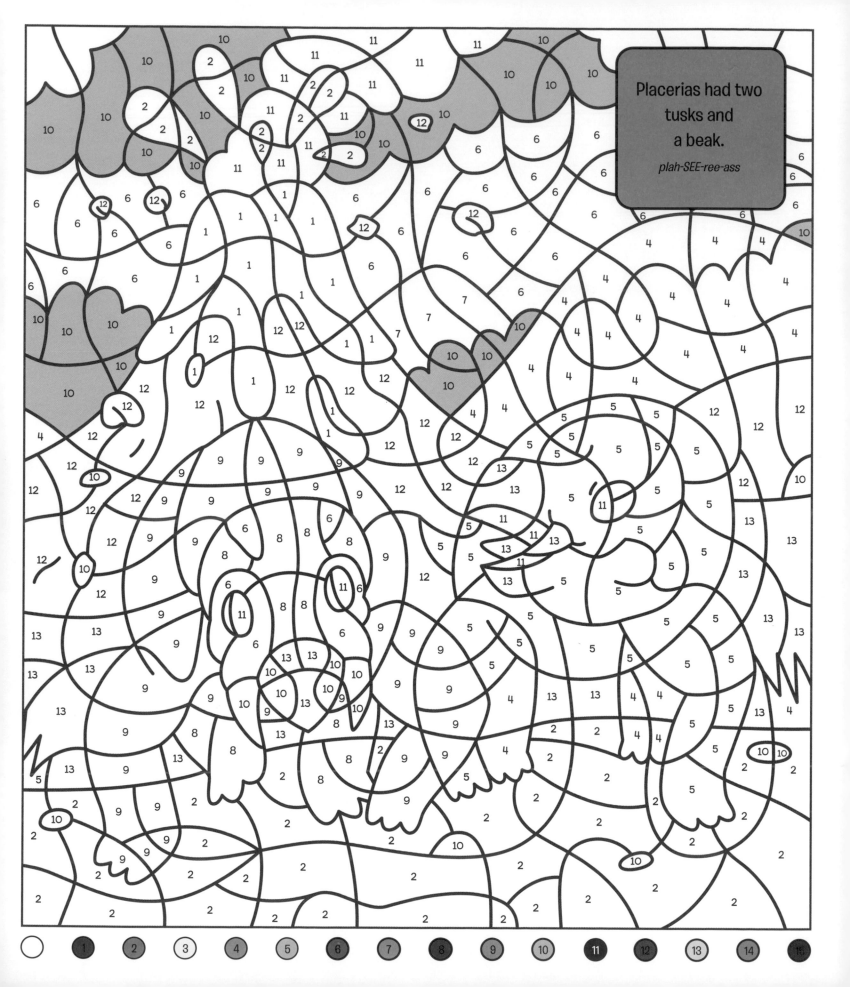

Placerias had two tusks and a beak.

plah-SEE-ree-ass

Albertonectes
had a rather long neck.

al-BERT-oh-nec-tes

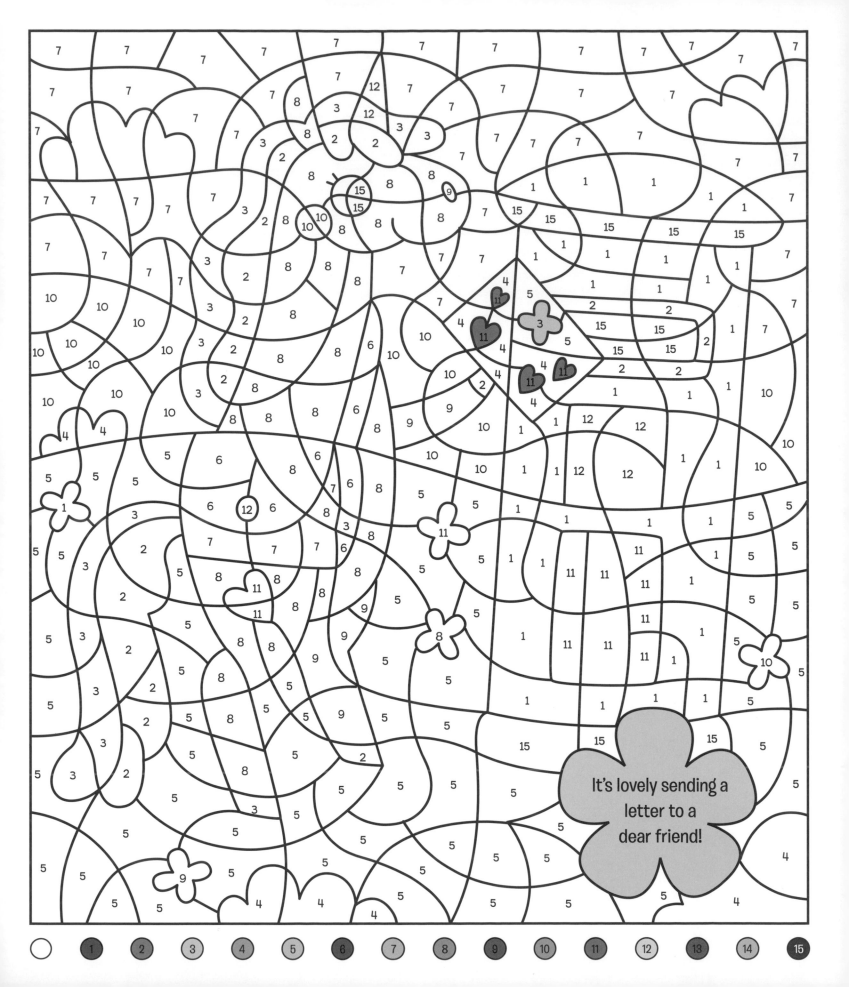

It's lovely sending a letter to a dear friend!

Under the sea is the perfect home for me!

These little finches love to sing.

Quetzalcoatlus was a huge flying creature!

KWETS-ul-koh-AT-luss

Bird-like Troodons guarded their eggs.

TROH-oh-don

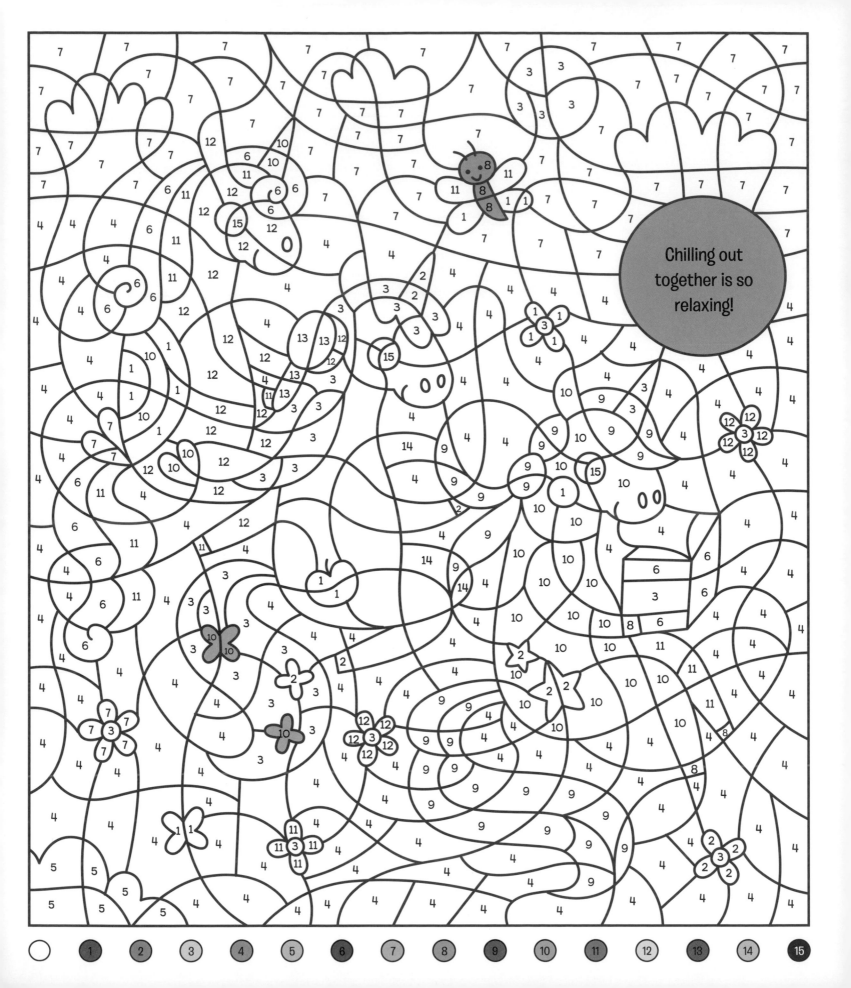

Everyone loves the candy store!

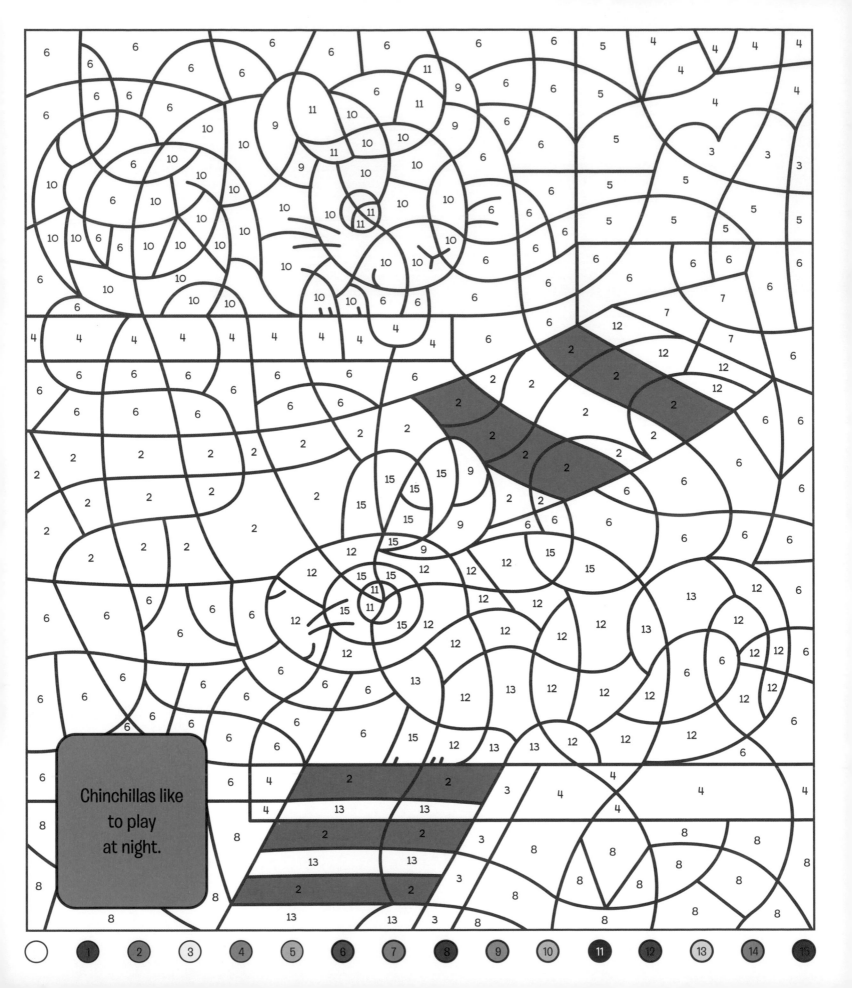

Chinchillas like to play at night.

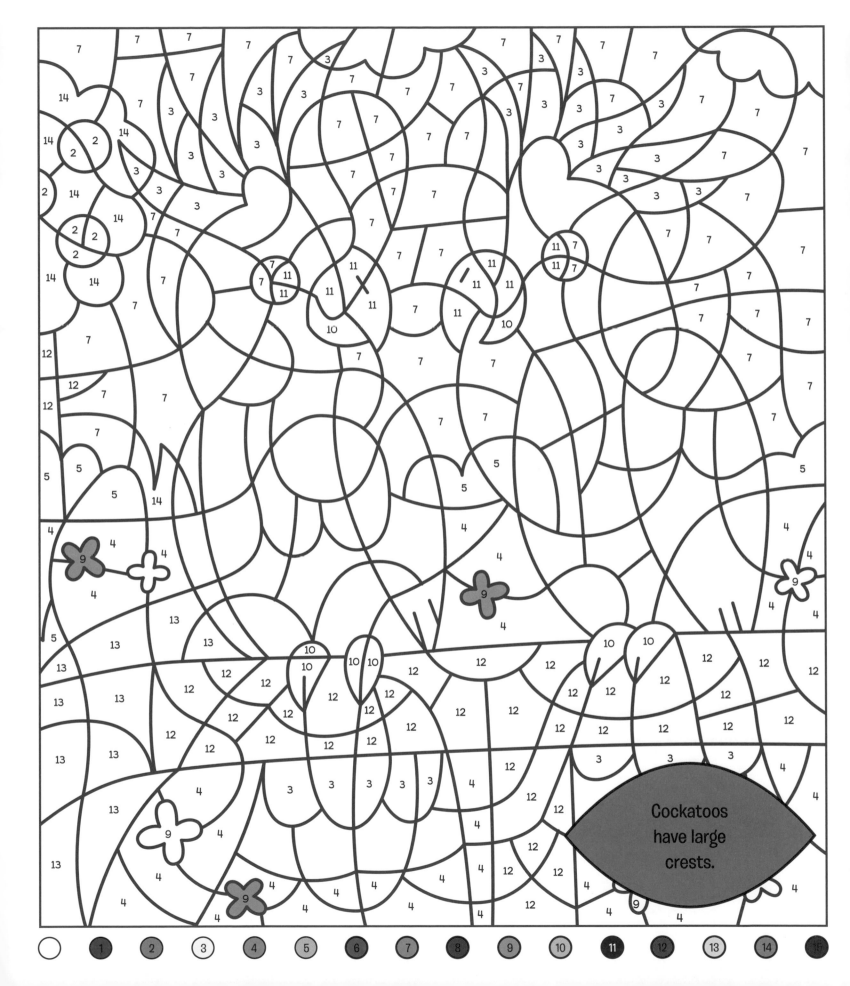

Cockatoos have large crests.

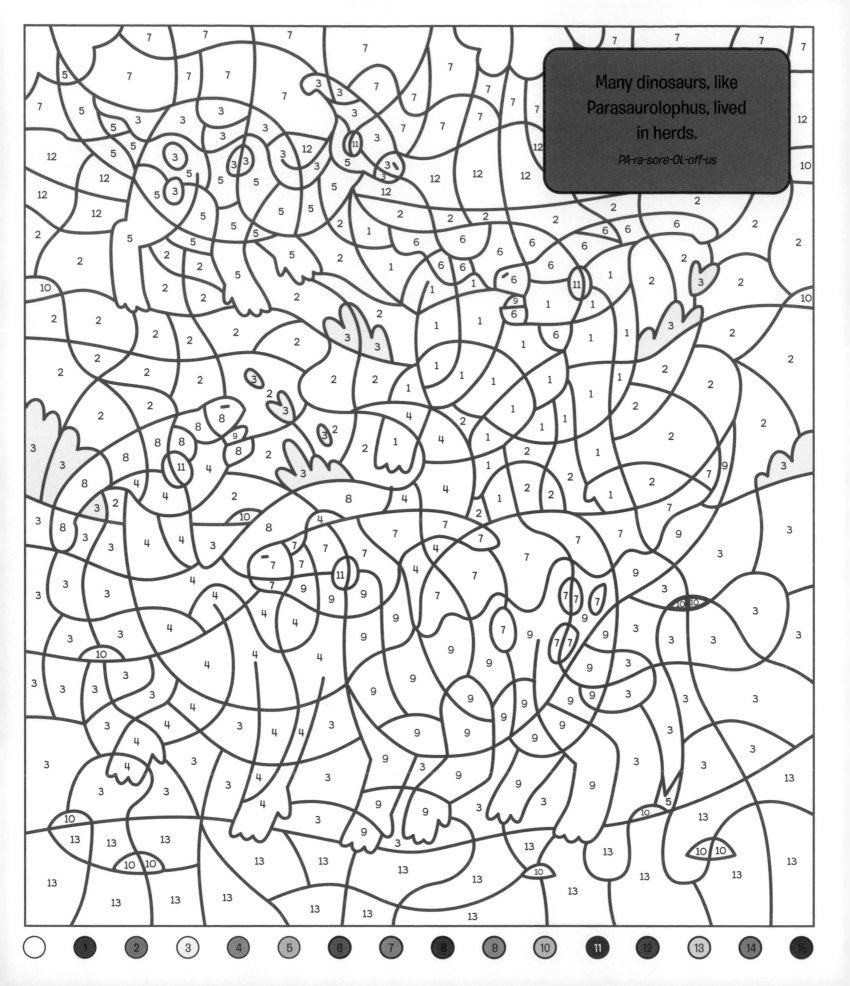

Many dinosaurs, like Parasaurolophus, lived in herds.

PA-ra-sore-OL-off-us

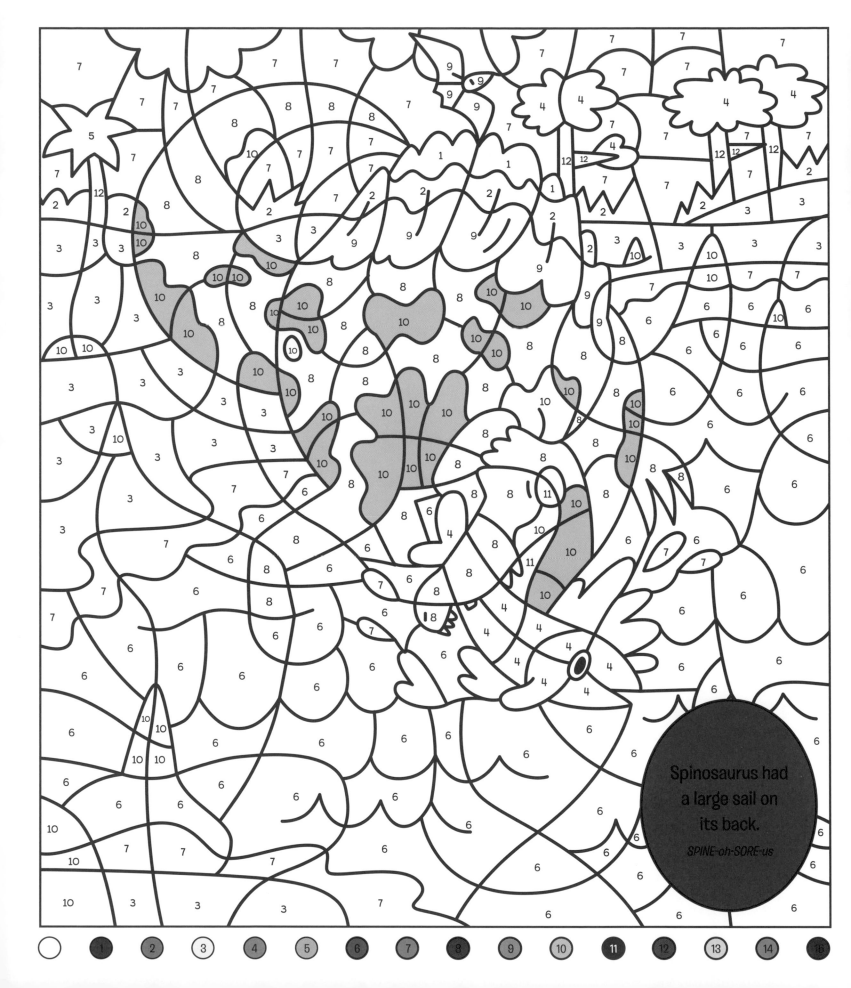

Spinosaurus had a large sail on its back.

SPINE-oh-SORE-us

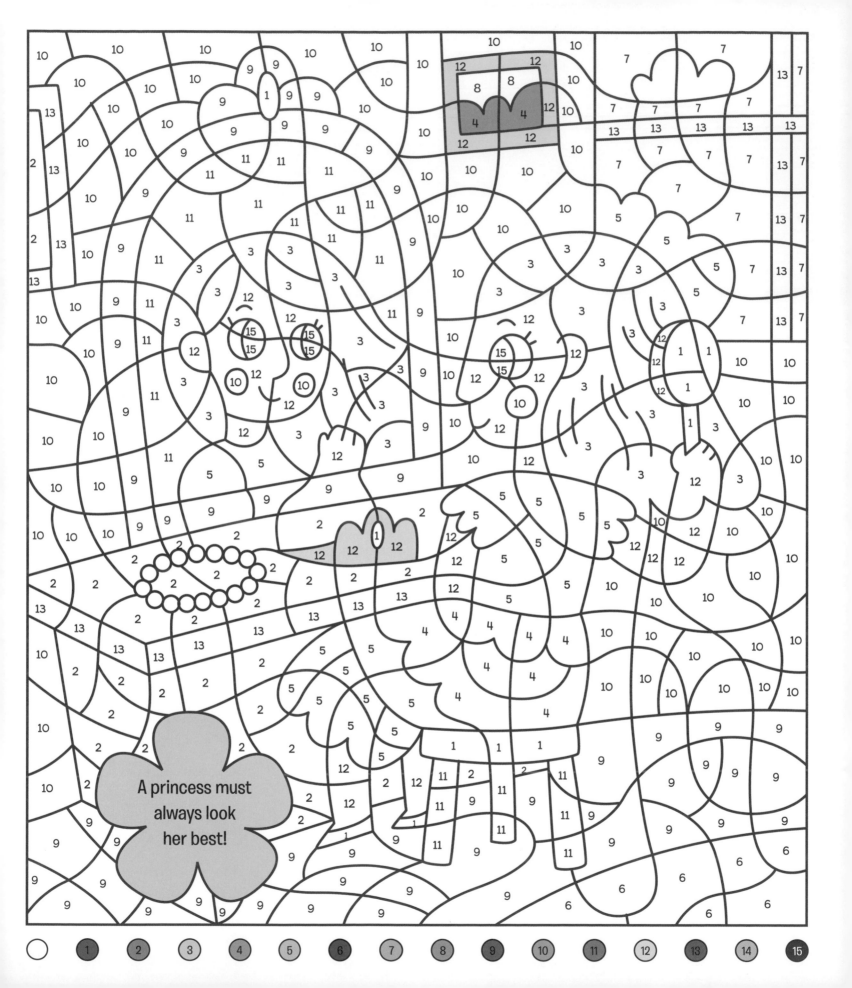

A princess must always look her best!

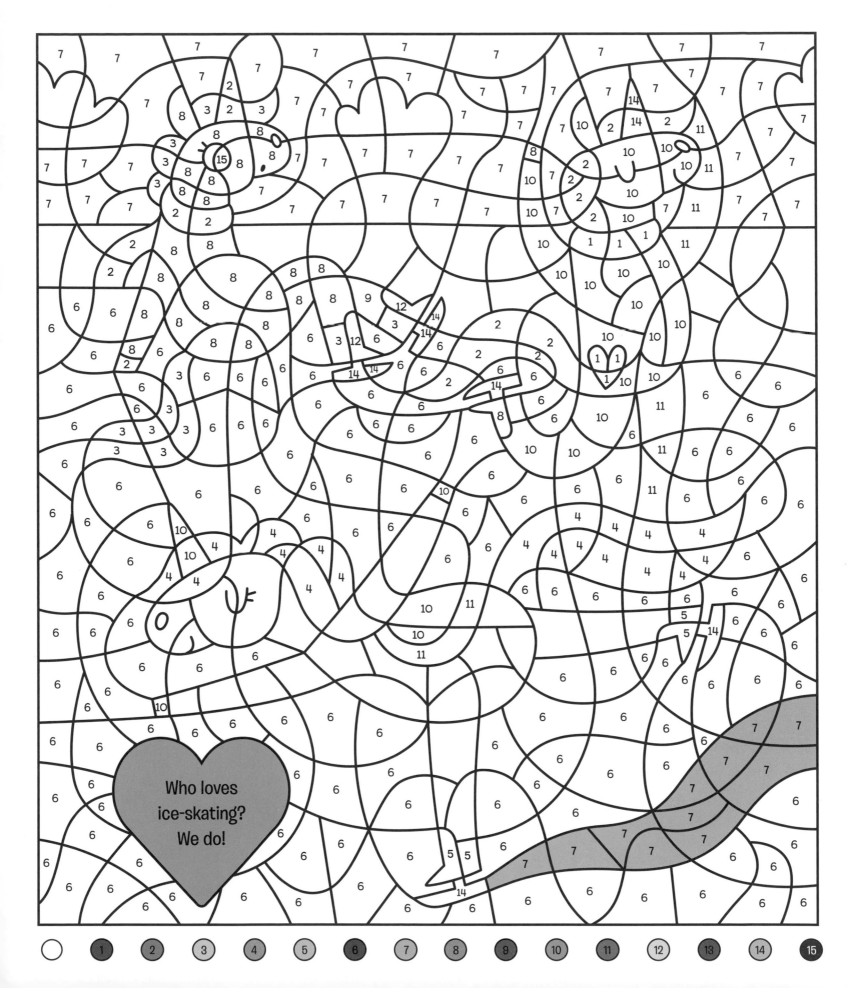

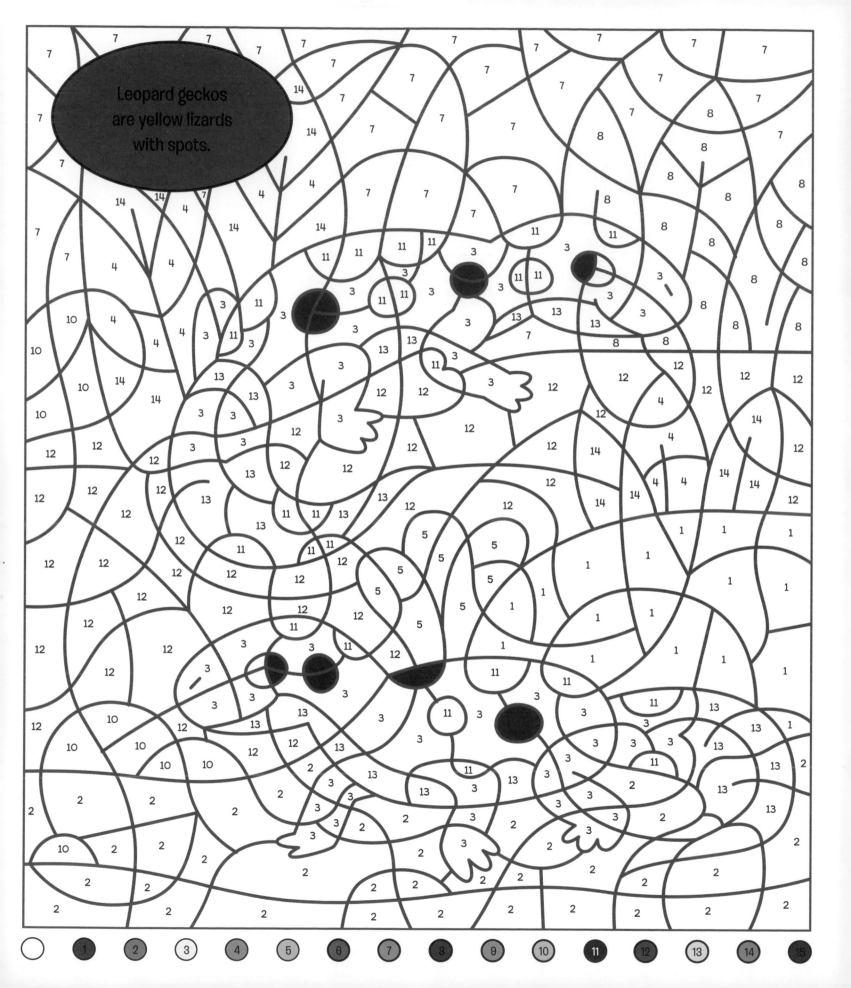

Greyhounds can run very fast.

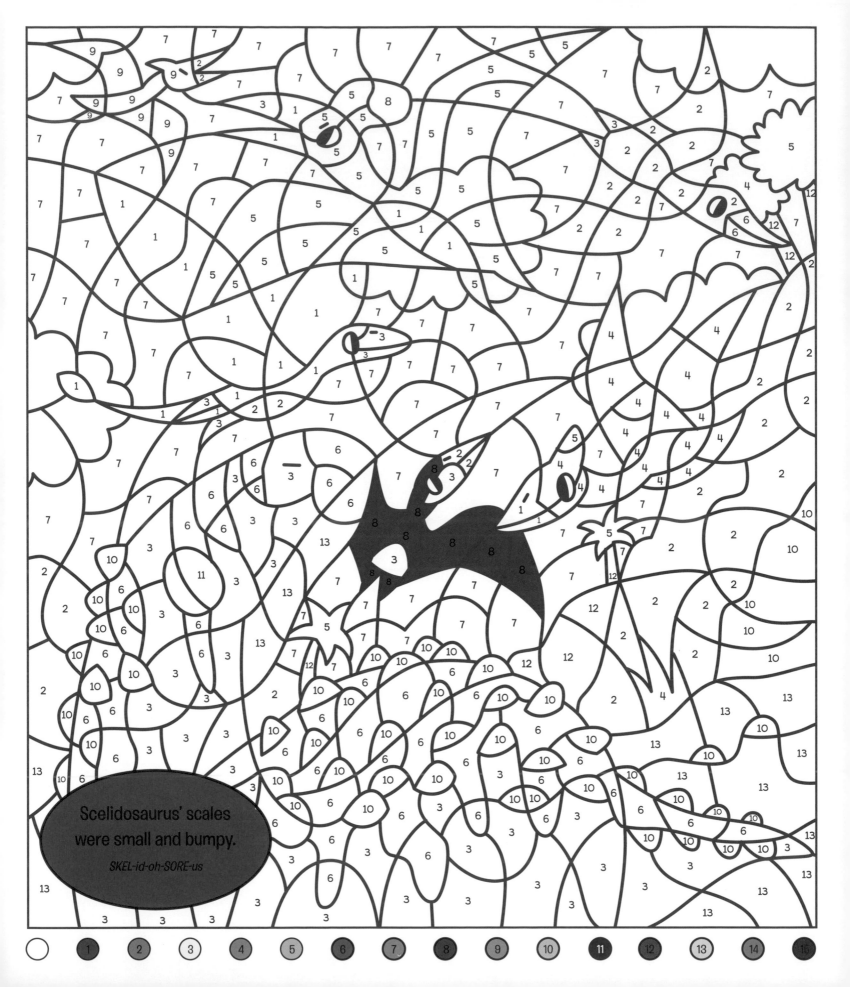

Scelidosaurus' scales were small and bumpy.

SKEL-id-oh-SORE-us

Be careful, Centrosaurus. You are being watched!

SEN-tro-SORE-us

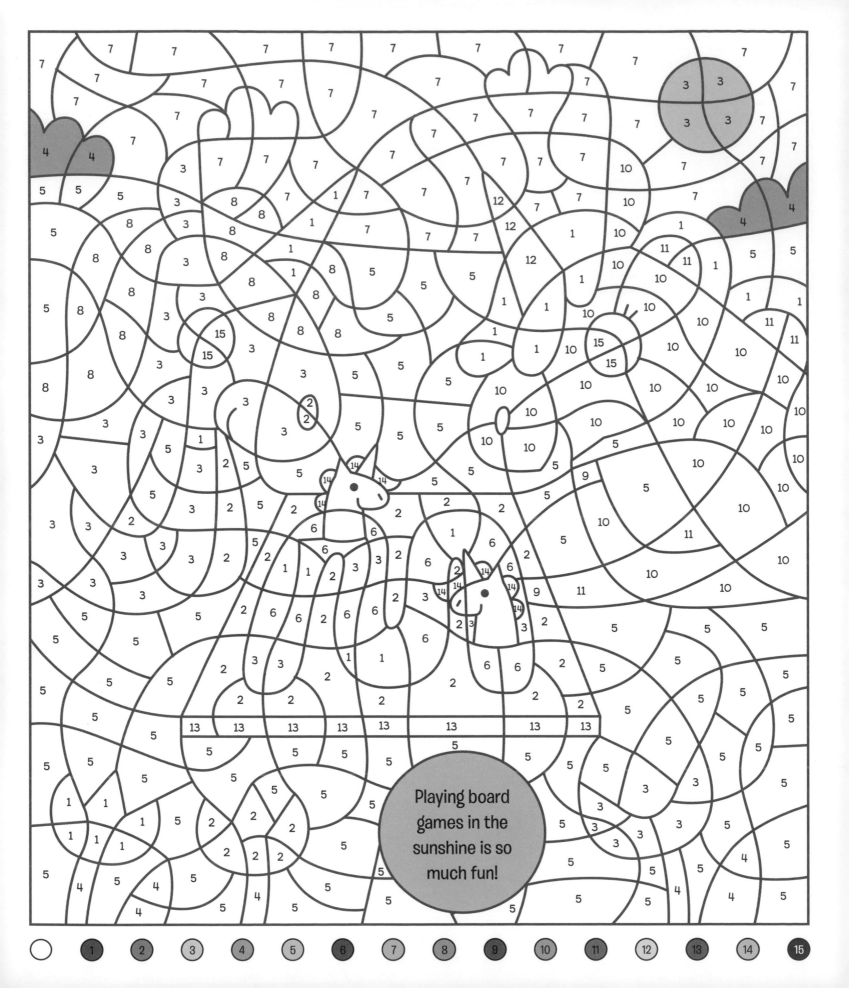

Playing board games in the sunshine is so much fun!

It's time to cast a spell!

Chameleons have bumpy scales.

The baby ostrich has just hatched.

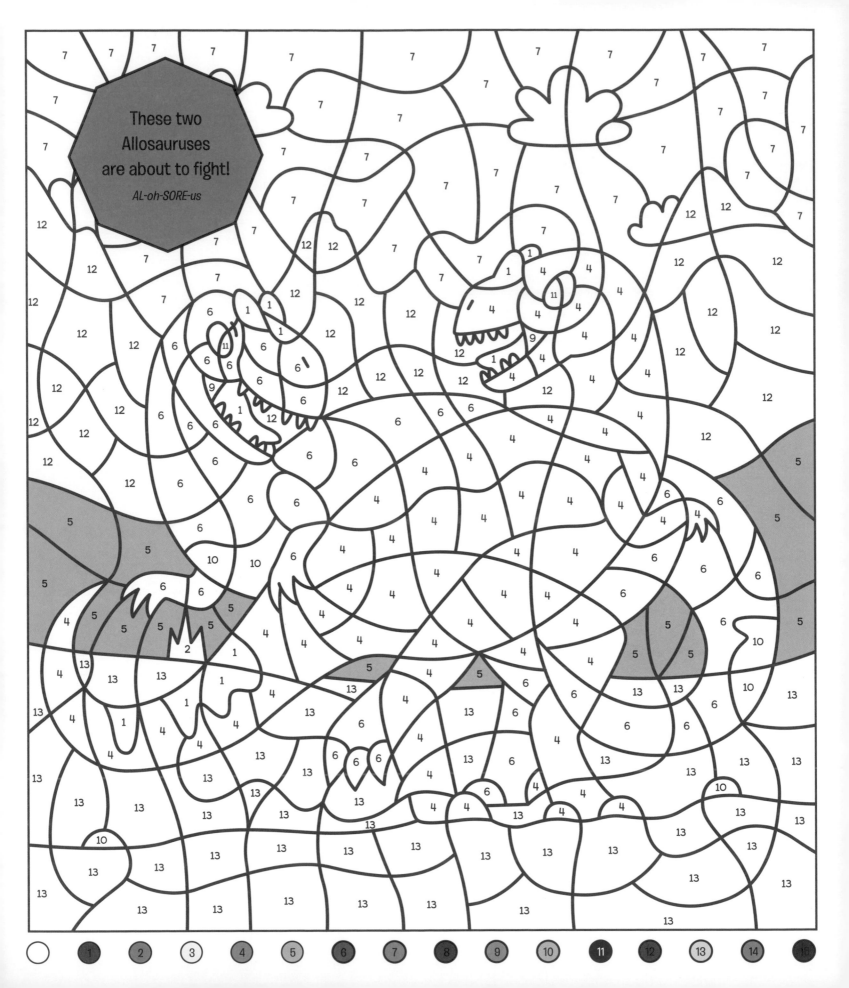

These two Allosauruses are about to fight!

AL-oh-SORE-us

Gastonia had bony spikes on its back.

gas-TOH-nee-ah

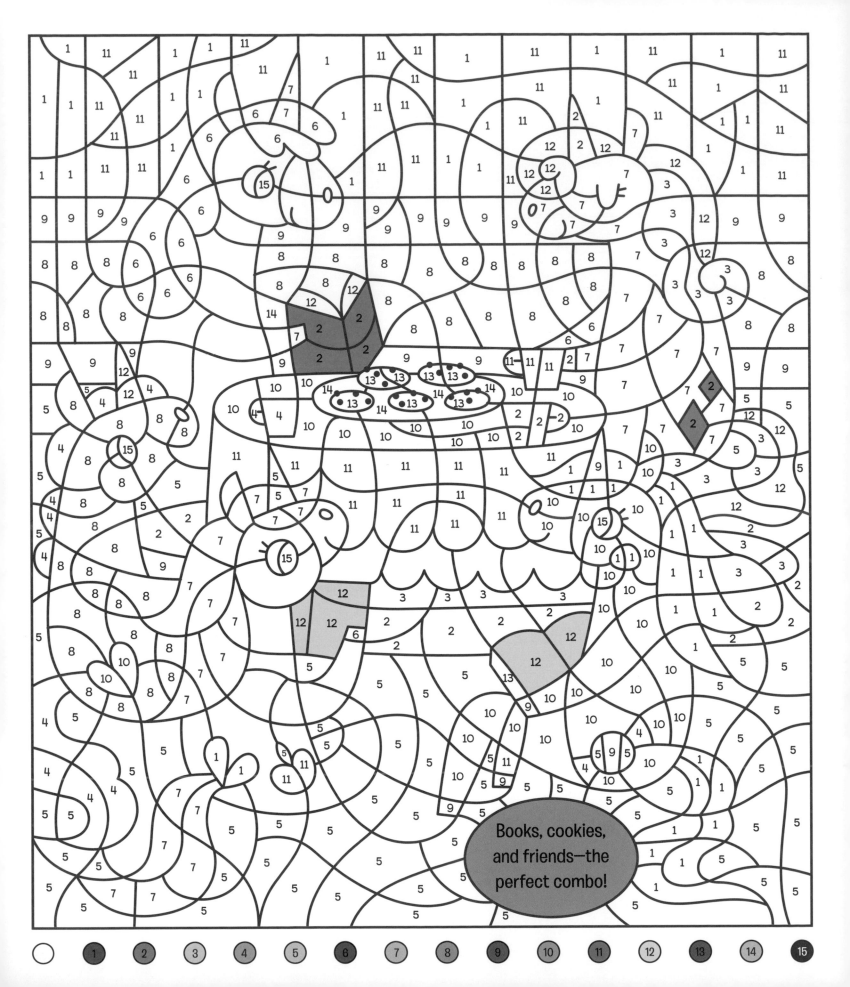

Books, cookies, and friends—the perfect combo!

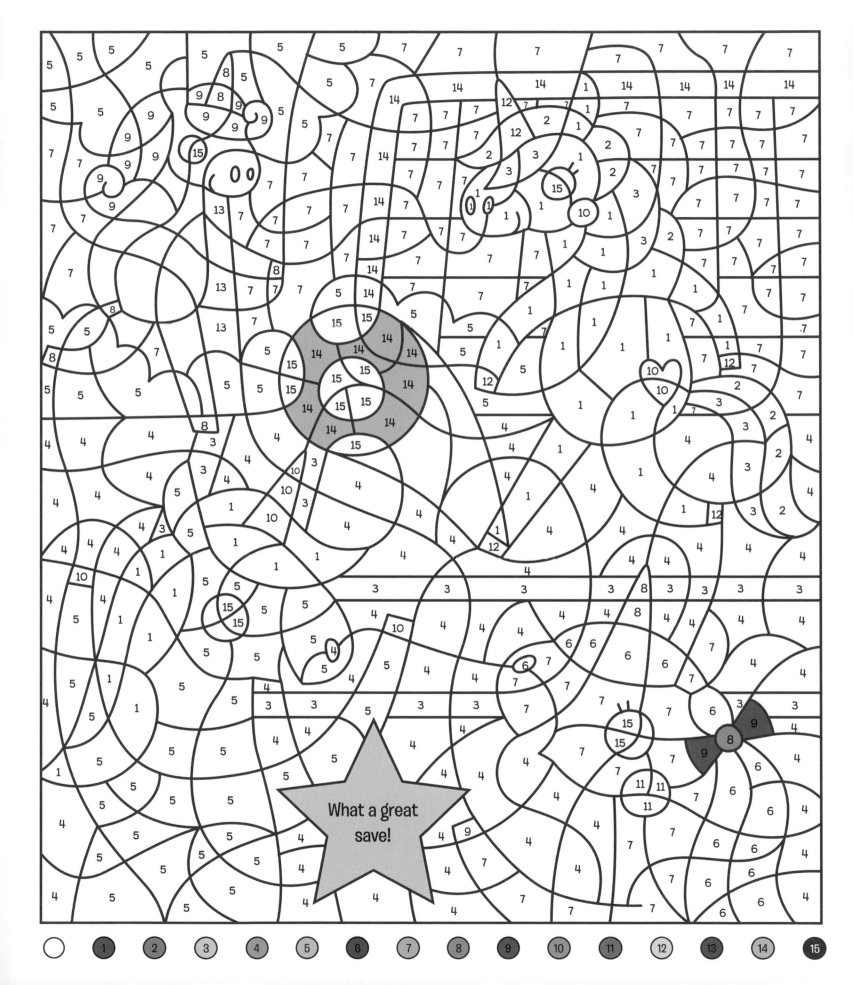

What a great save!

Teddy bear hamsters have very long fur.

Red-eyed tree frogs eat bugs.

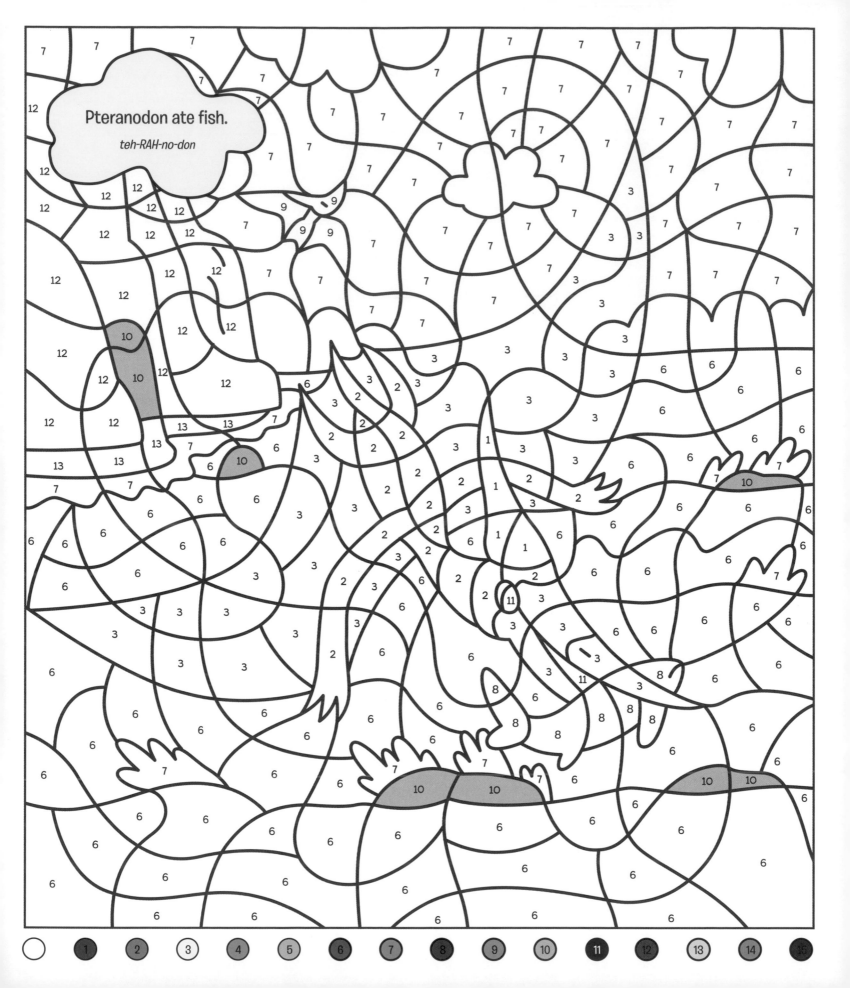

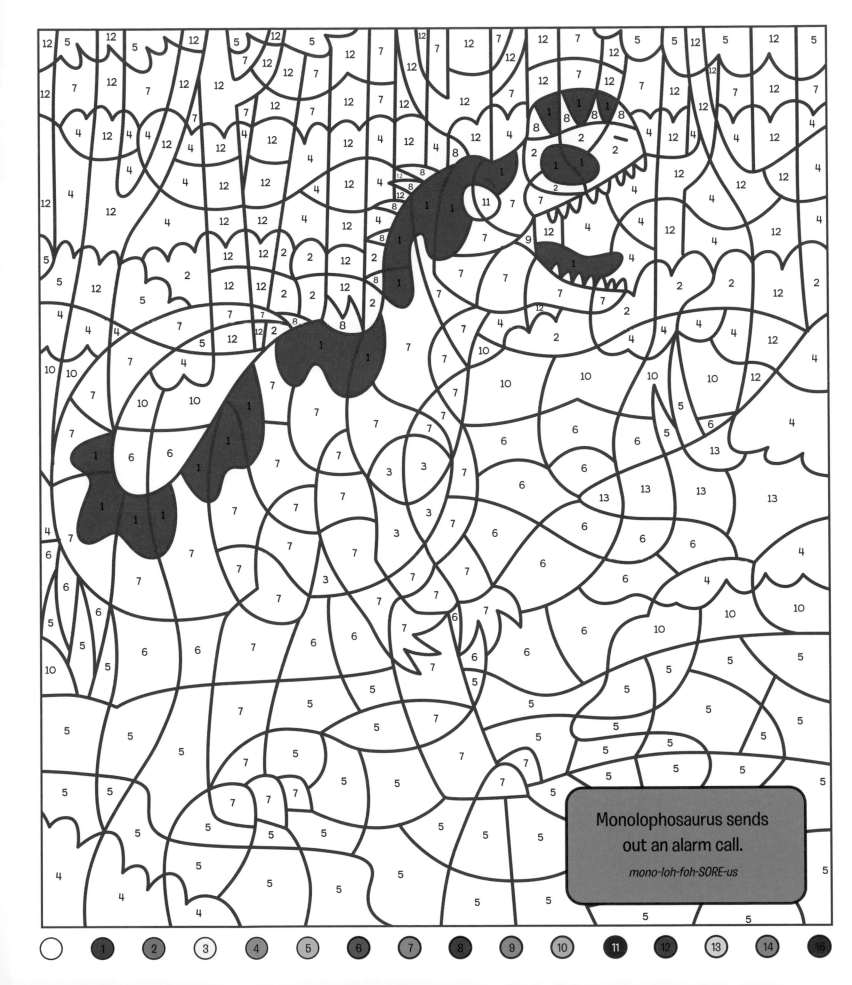

Monolophosaurus sends
out an alarm call.

mono-loh-foh-SORE-us

Growing fruit and vegetables is fun!

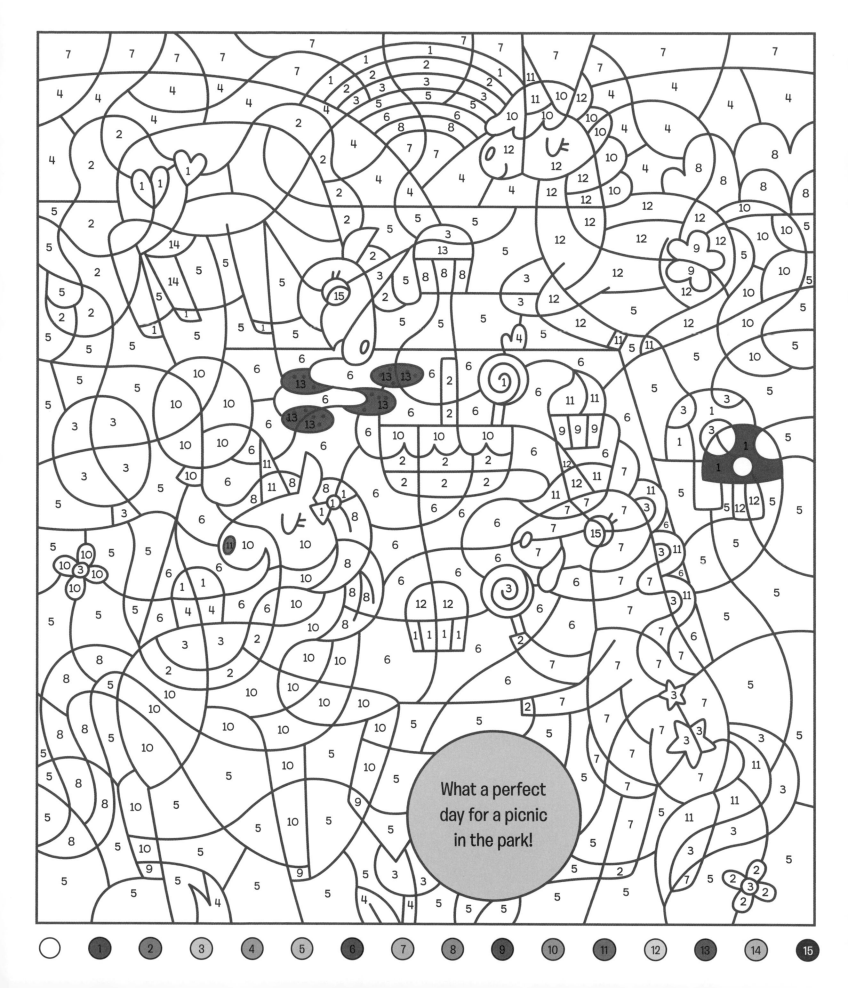

What a perfect day for a picnic in the park!

Pet tarantulas have eight hairy legs.

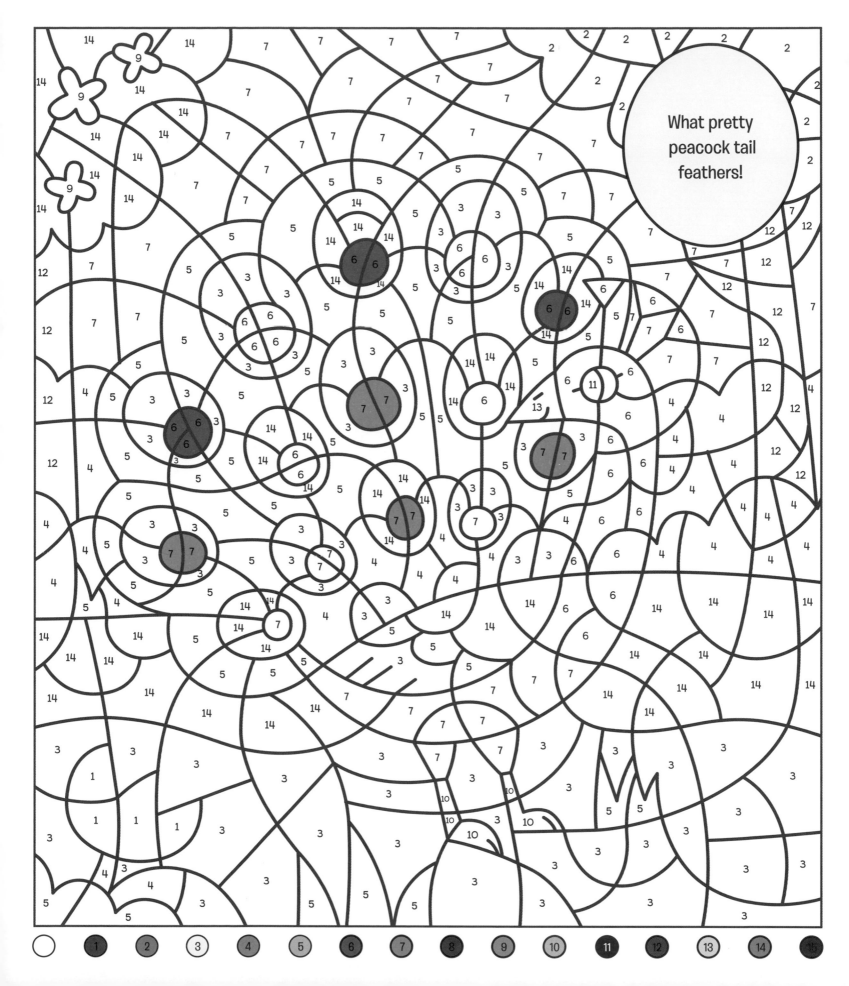

What pretty peacock tail feathers!

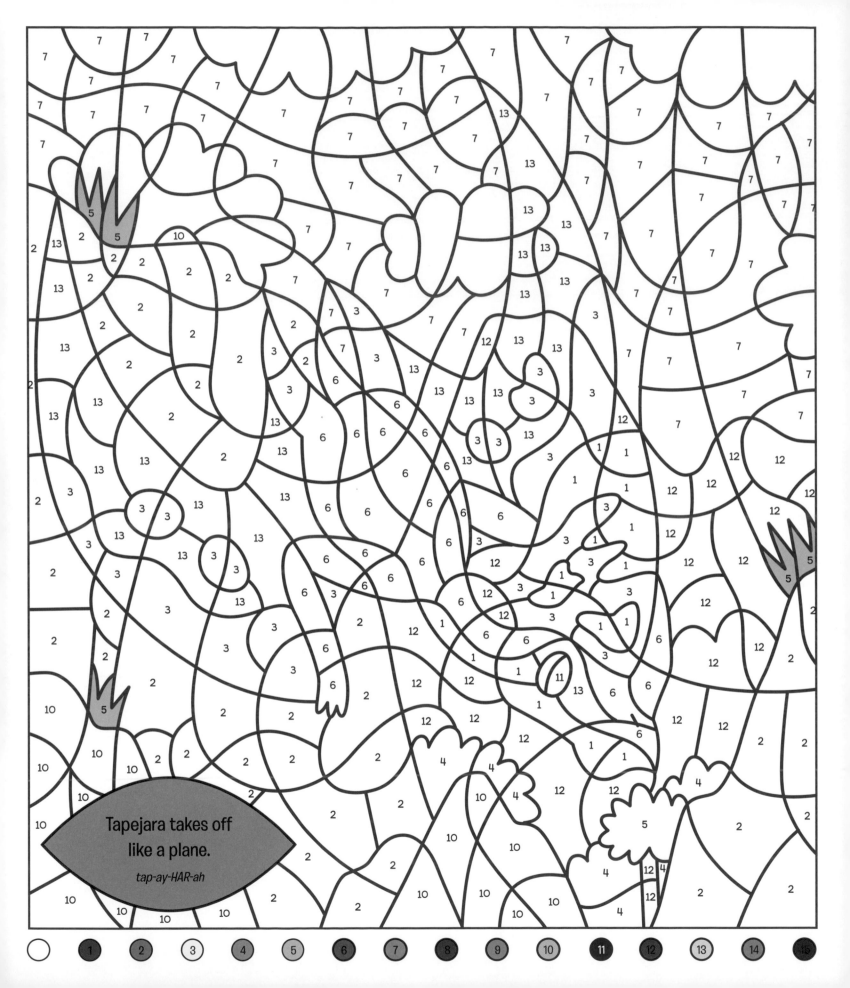

Tapejara takes off
like a plane.

tap-ay-HAR-ah

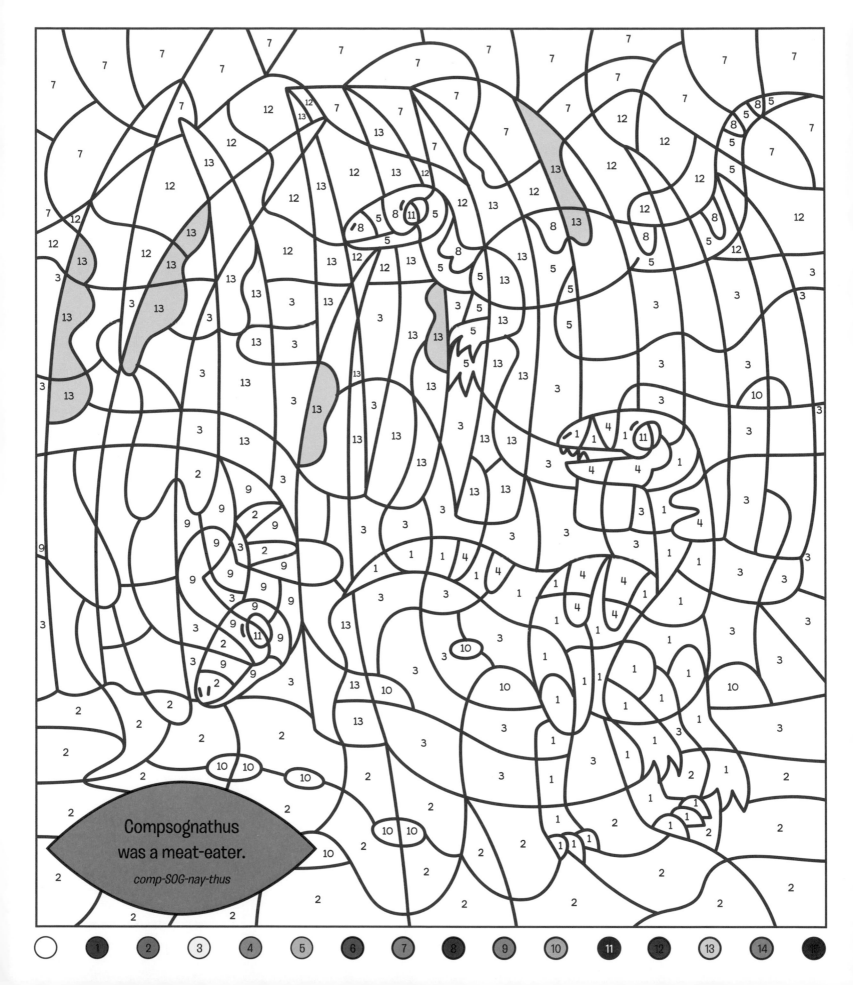

Compsognathus
was a meat-eater.

comp-SOG-nay-thus

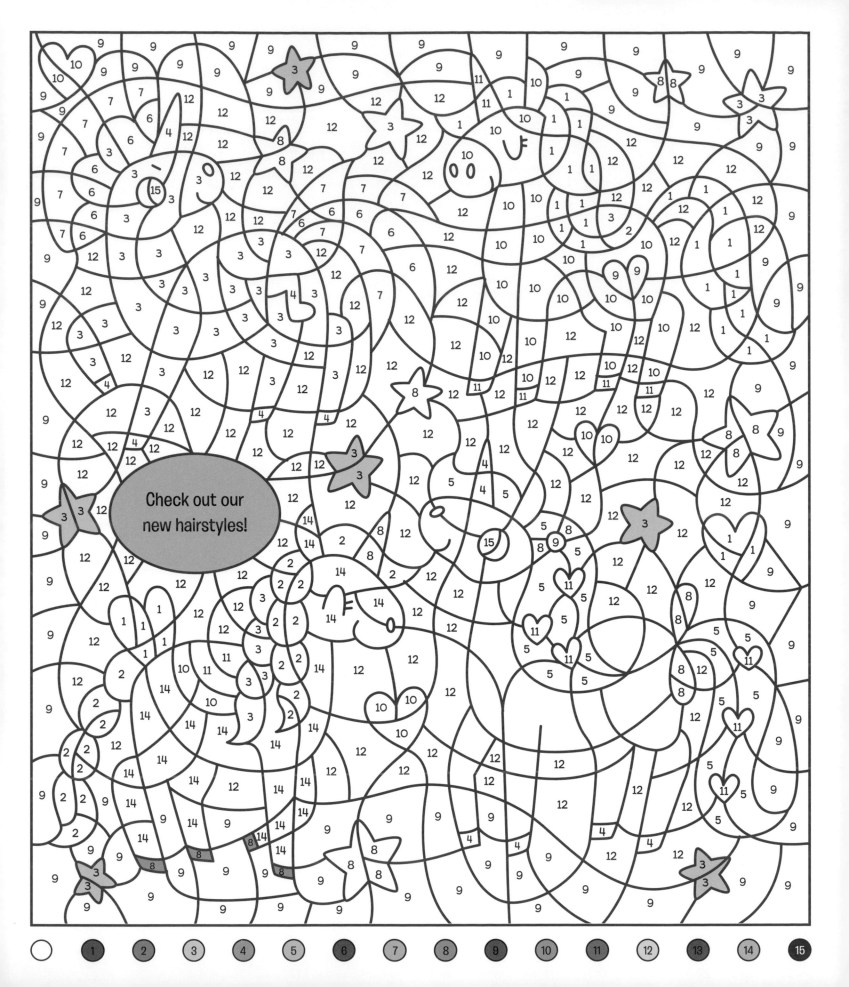

What a lovely day
for a carriage ride!

Dormice have long and furry tails.

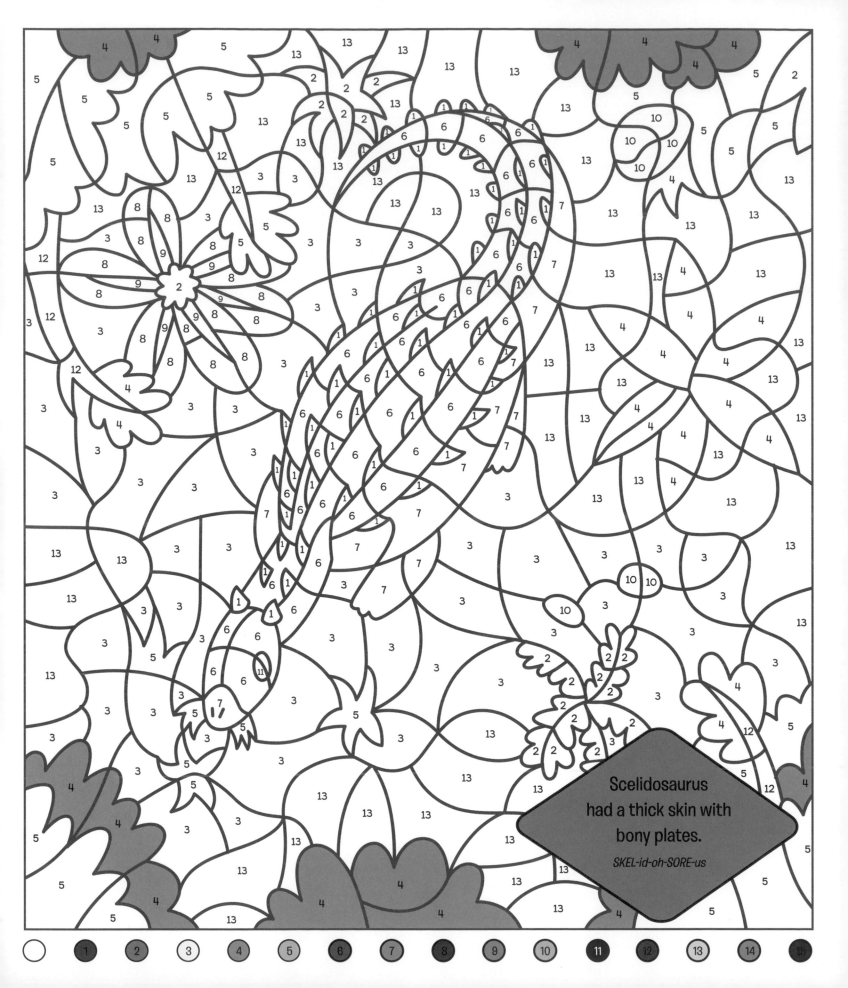

Scelidosaurus had a thick skin with bony plates.

SKEL-id-oh-SORE-us

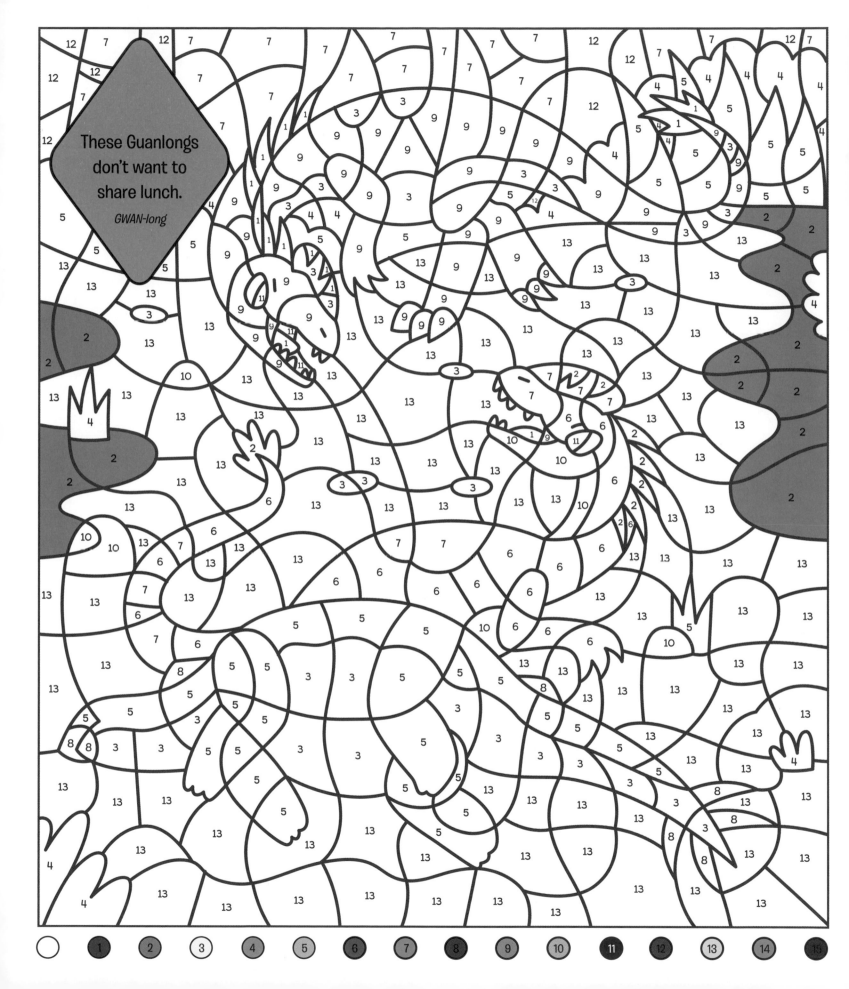

These Guanlongs don't want to share lunch.

GWAN-long

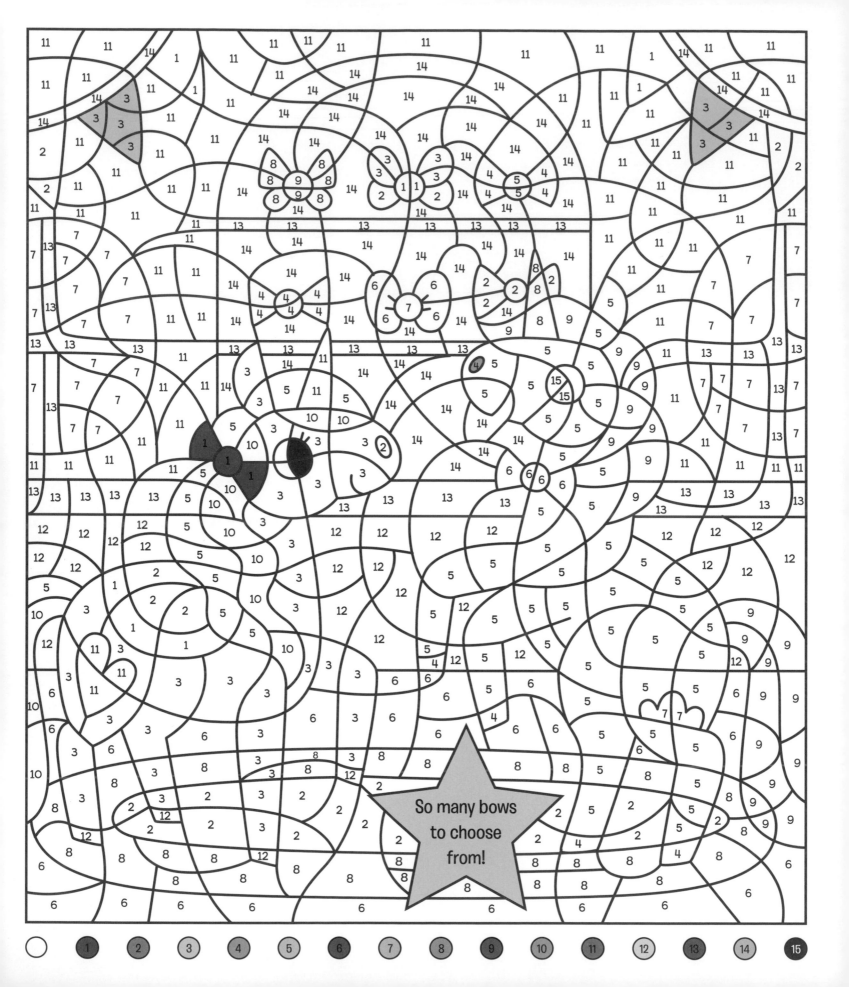

So many bows to choose from!

Wrap up warm, it's time to build a snow-unicorn!

Bengal cats have soft and silky coats.

This horse likes juicy red apples.

Brachiosaurus was as tall as the trees!

BRAH-kee-oh-SORE-us

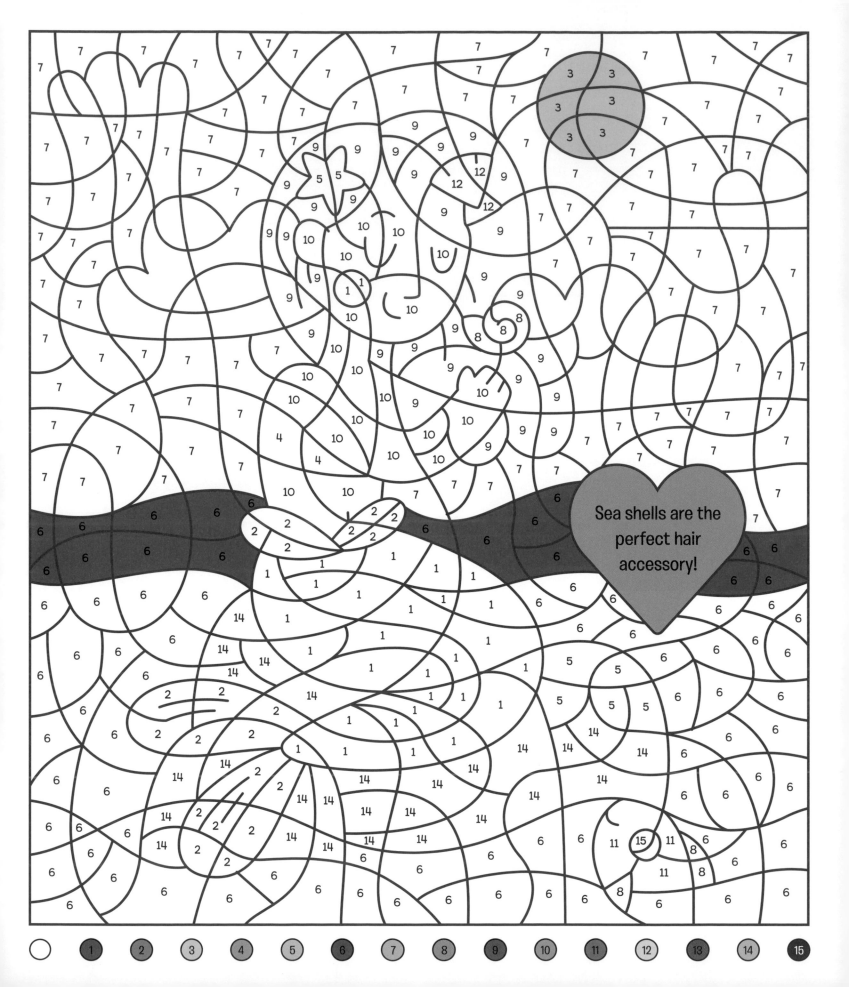

Sea shells are the perfect hair accessory!

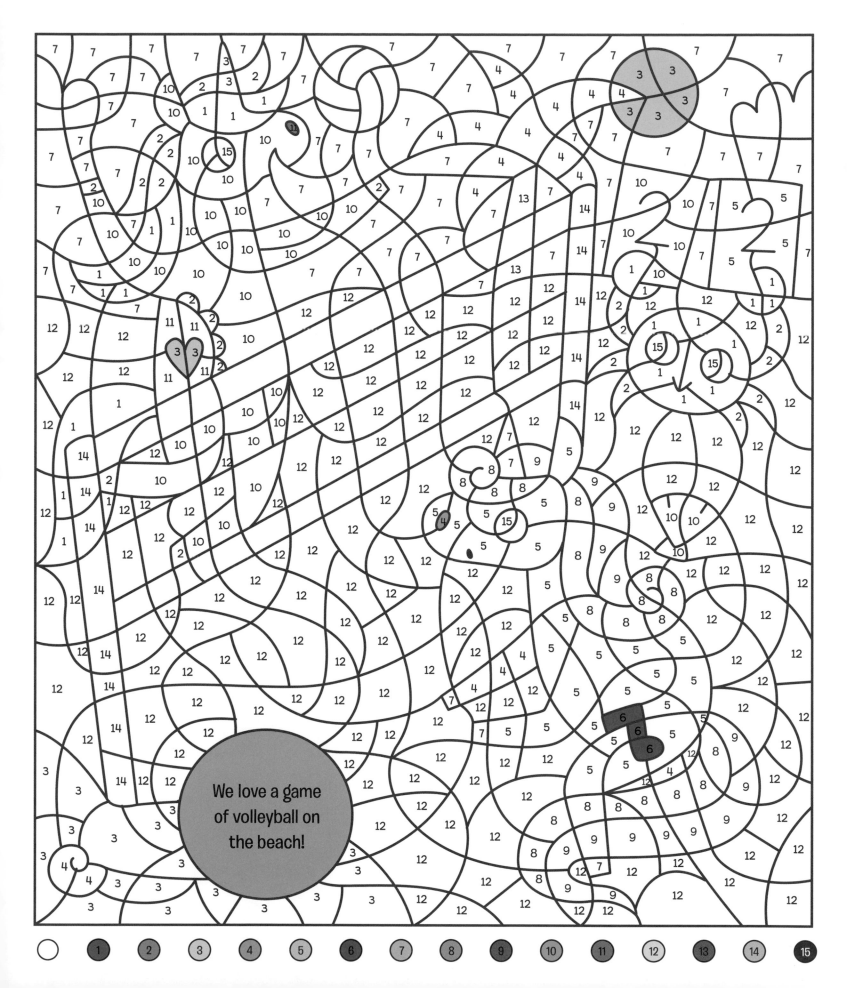

We love a game of volleyball on the beach!

How many baby bunnies can you see?

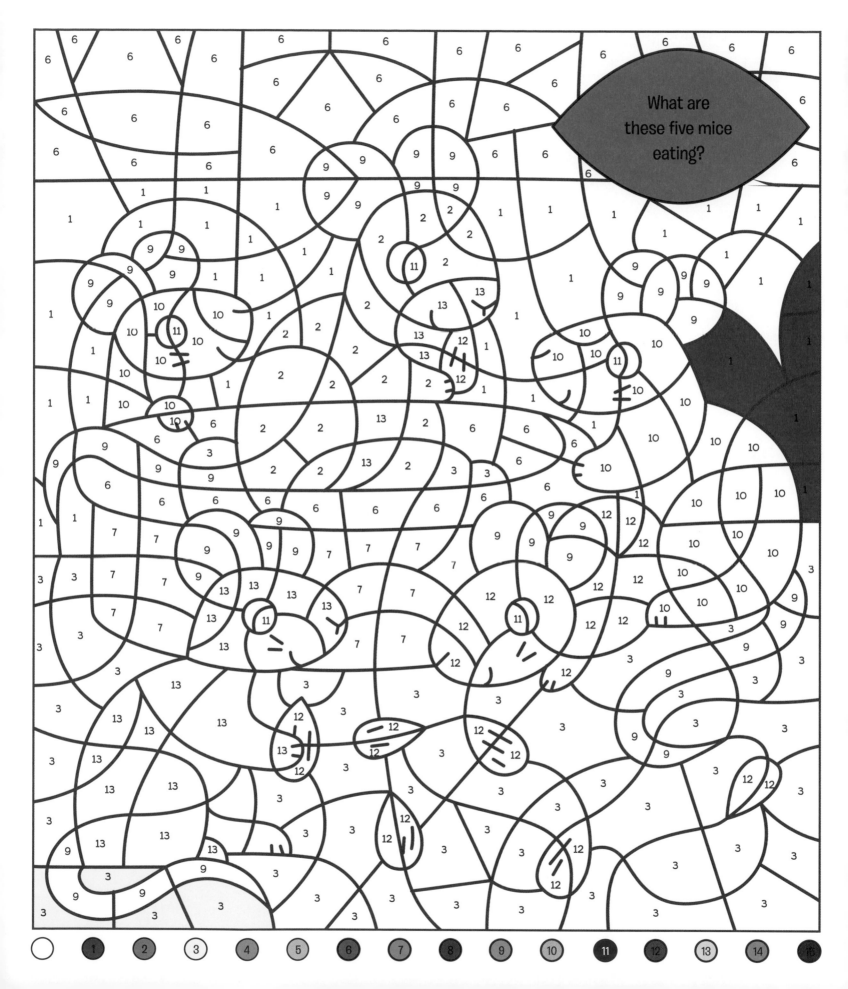

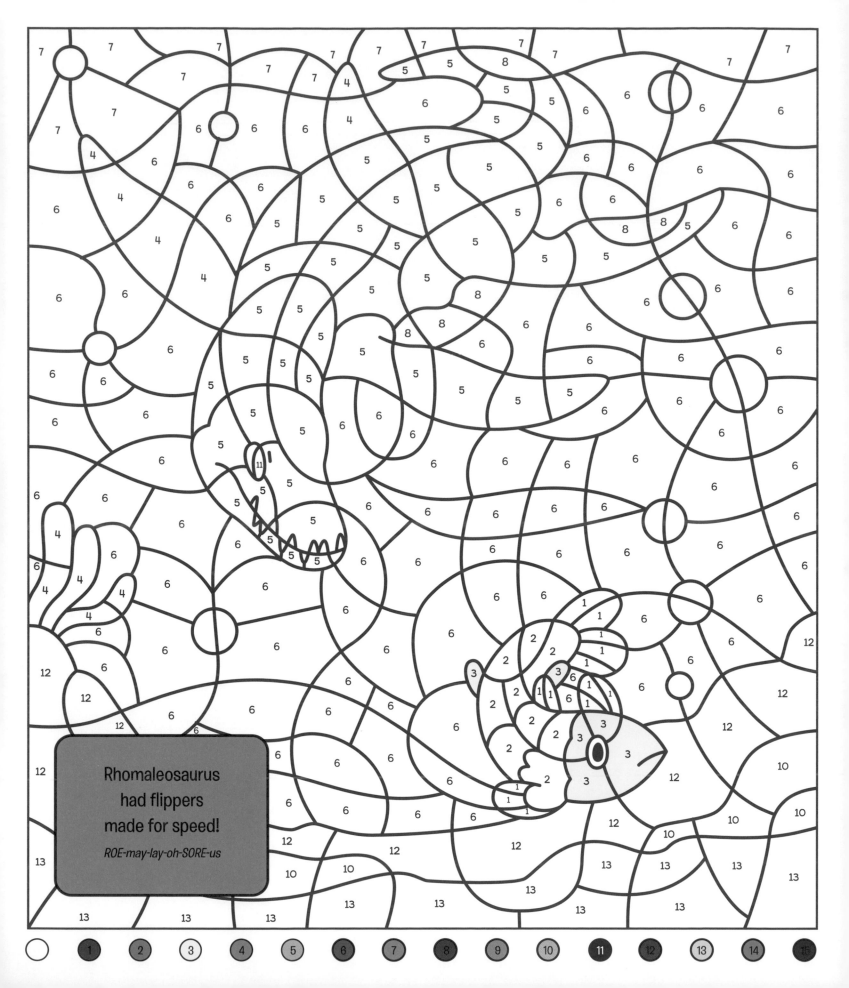

Rhomaleosaurus
had flippers
made for speed!

ROE-may-lay-oh-SORE-us

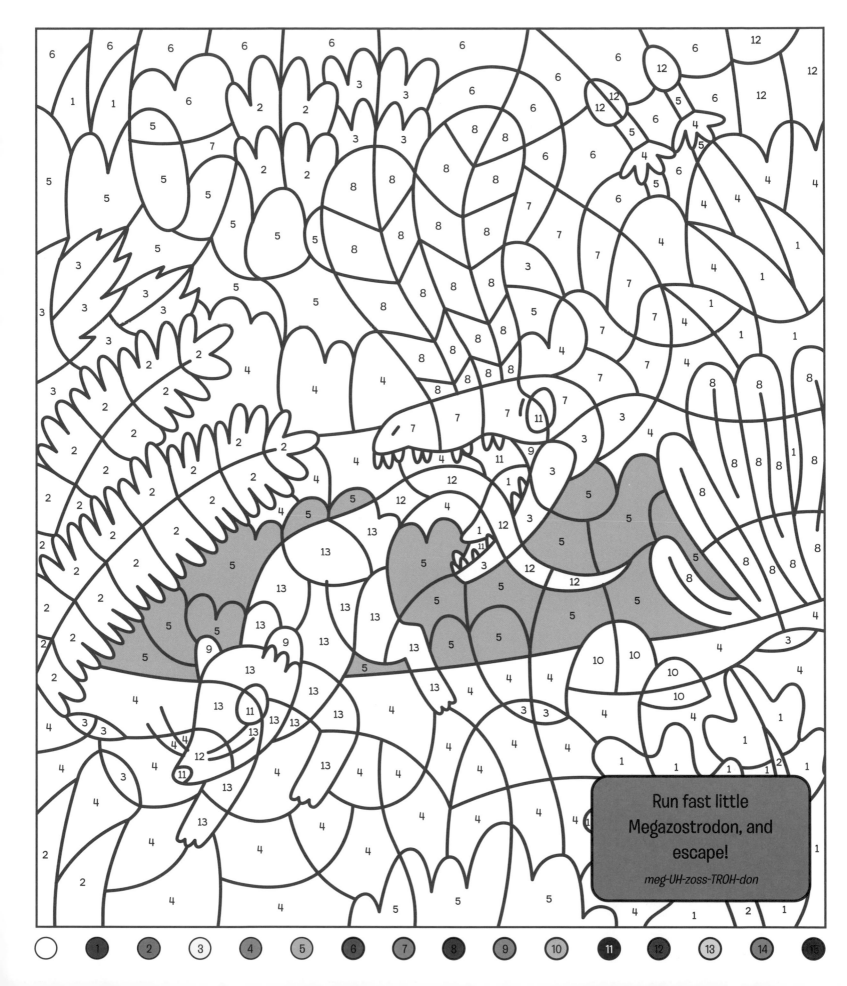

Run fast little Megazostrodon, and escape!

meg-UH-zoss-TROH-don

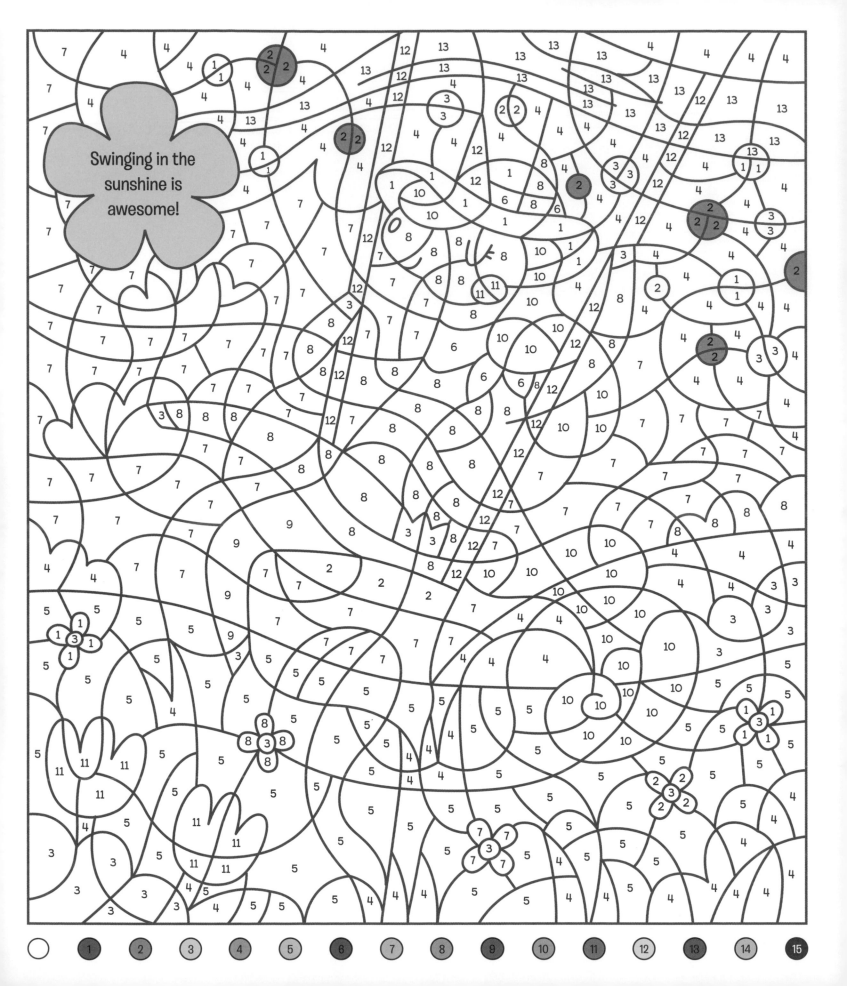

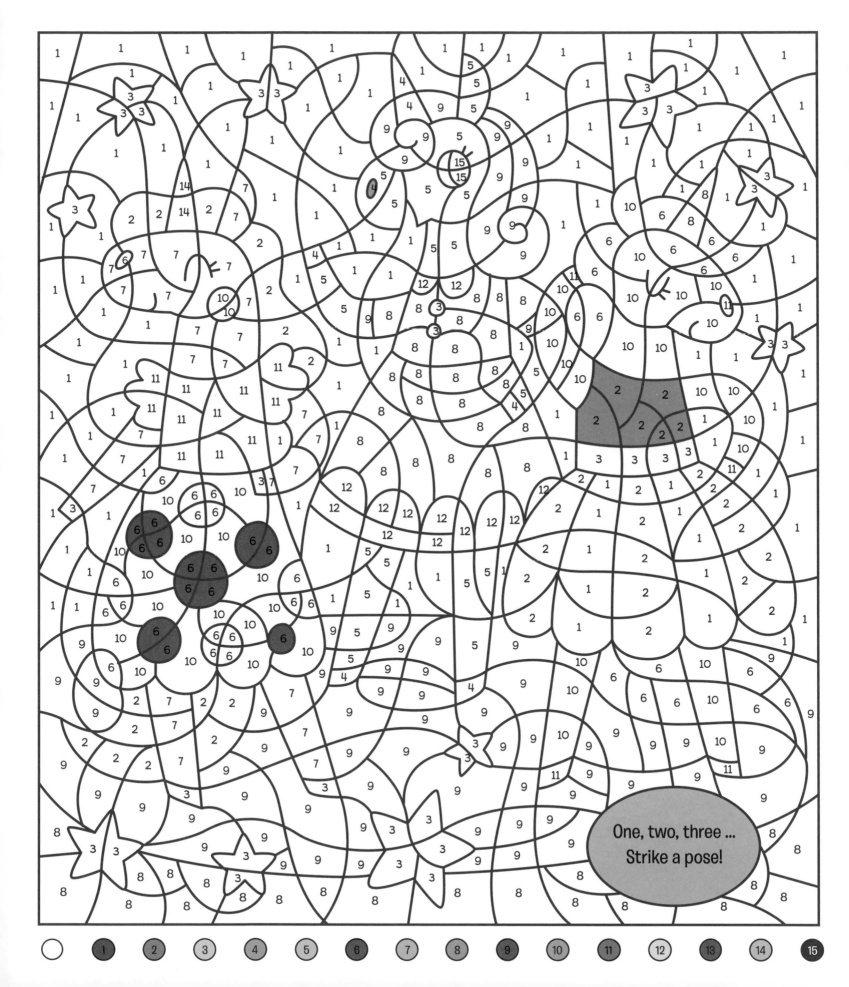

One, two, three ...
Strike a pose!

Huskies are good at pulling sleds.

Terrapins are tiny turtles.

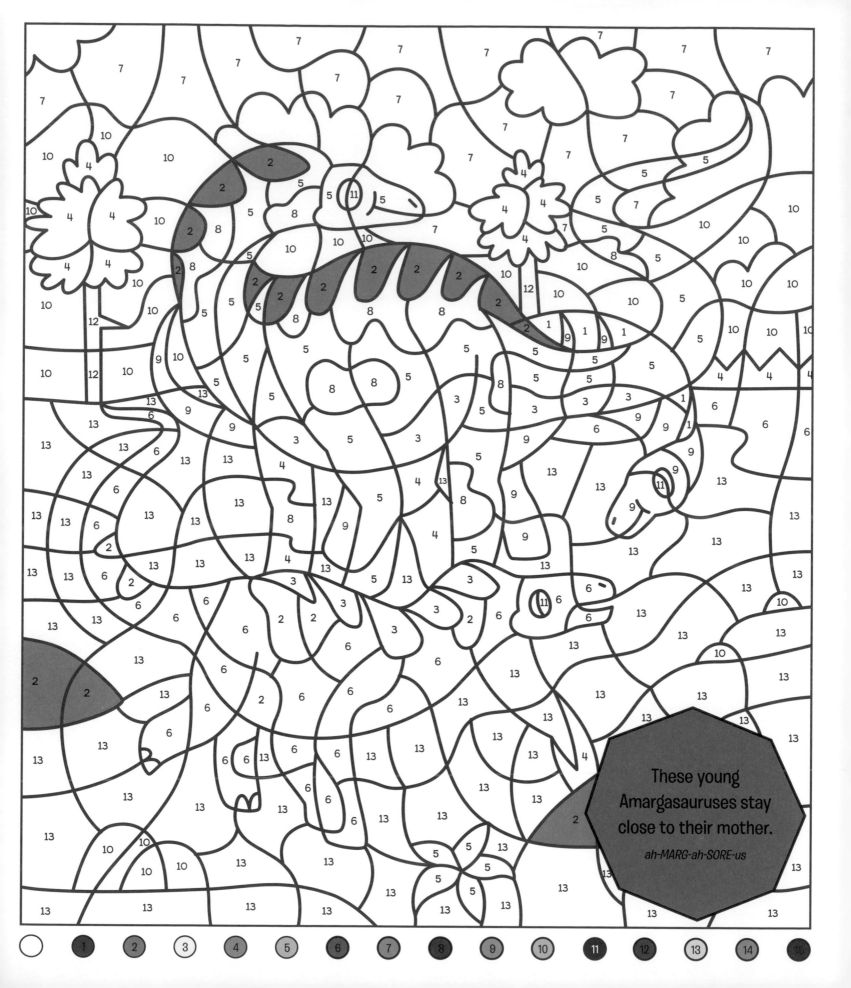

These young Amargasauruses stay close to their mother.

ah-MARG-ah-SORE-us

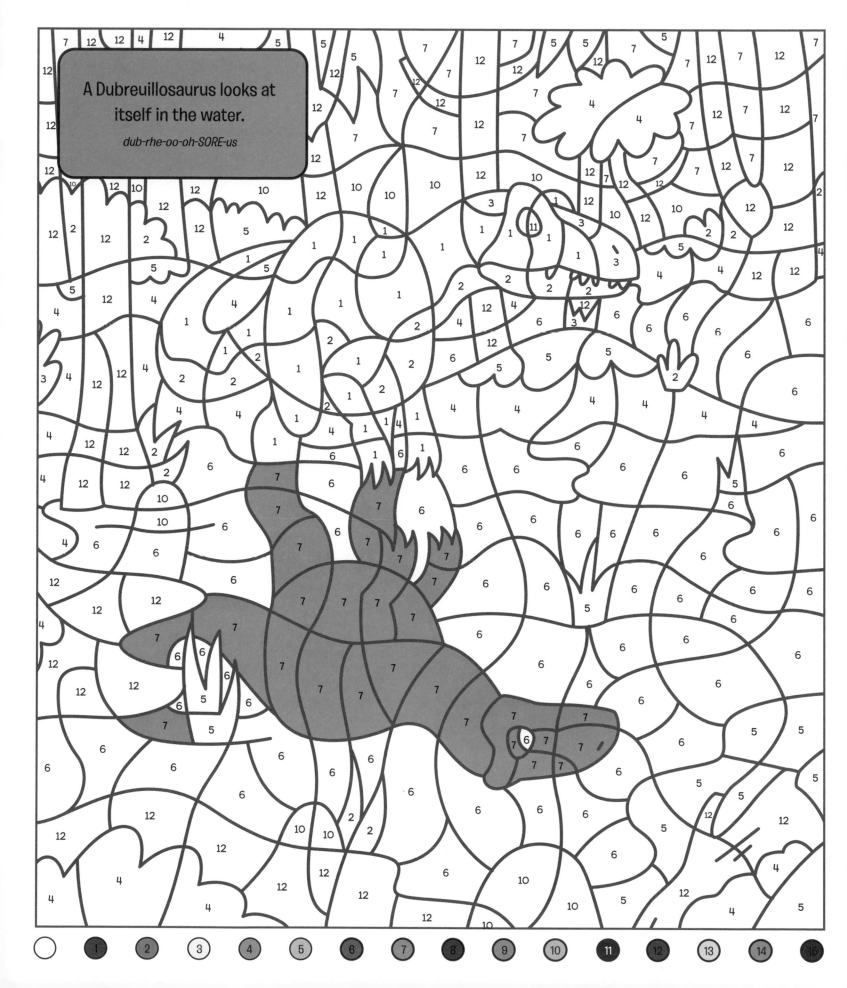

A Dubreuillosaurus looks at itself in the water.

dub-rhe-oo-oh-SORE-us

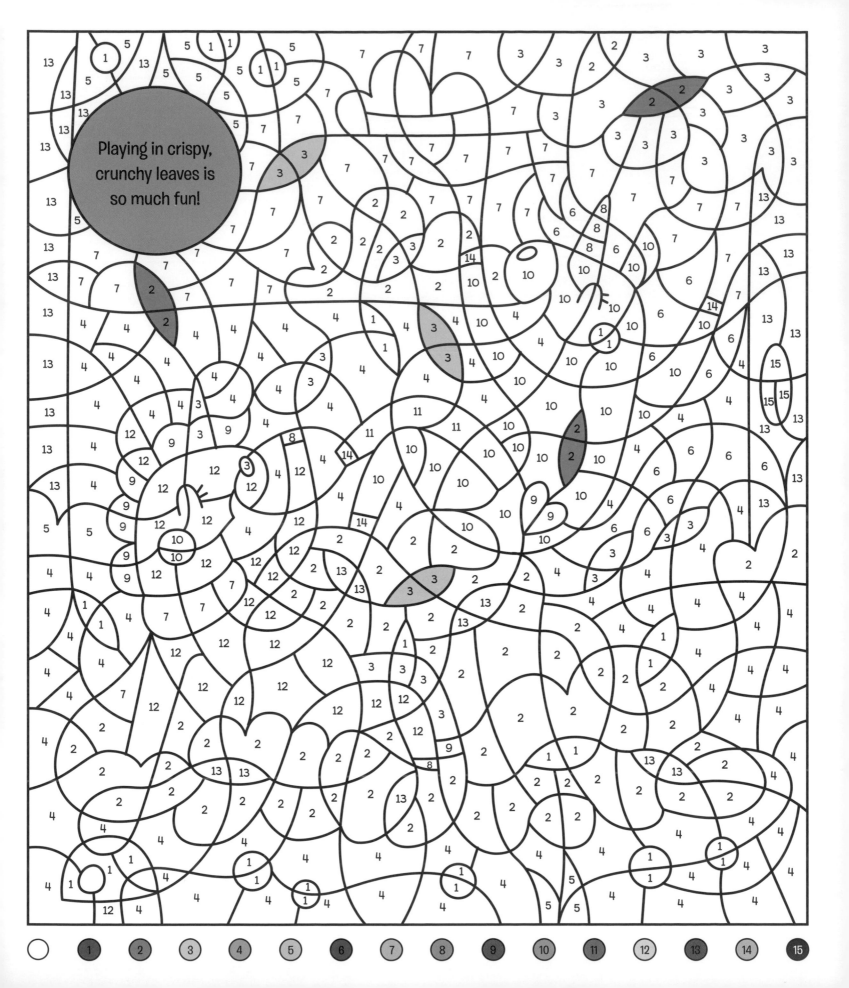

Playing in crispy, crunchy leaves is so much fun!

Nothing beats a good book and a warm fire!

Two strong oxen help the farmer in the field.

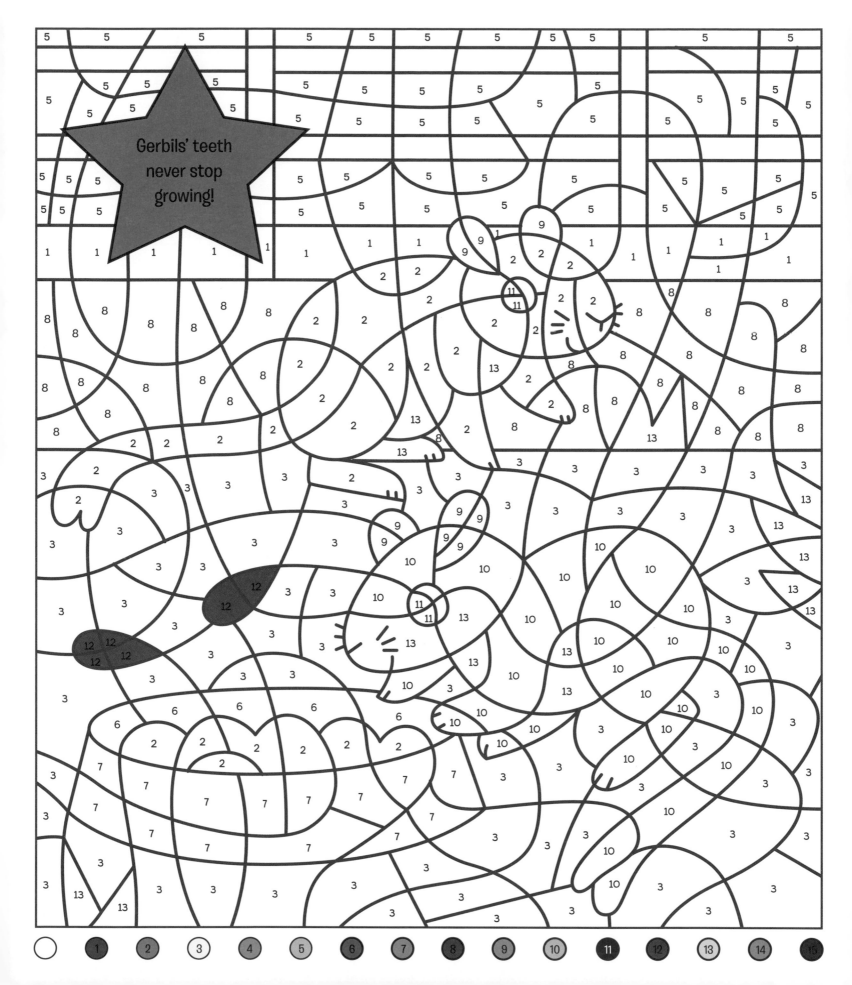

Gerbils' teeth never stop growing!

These Protoceratops are fleeing a forest fire.

PRO-toh-SEH-rah-tops

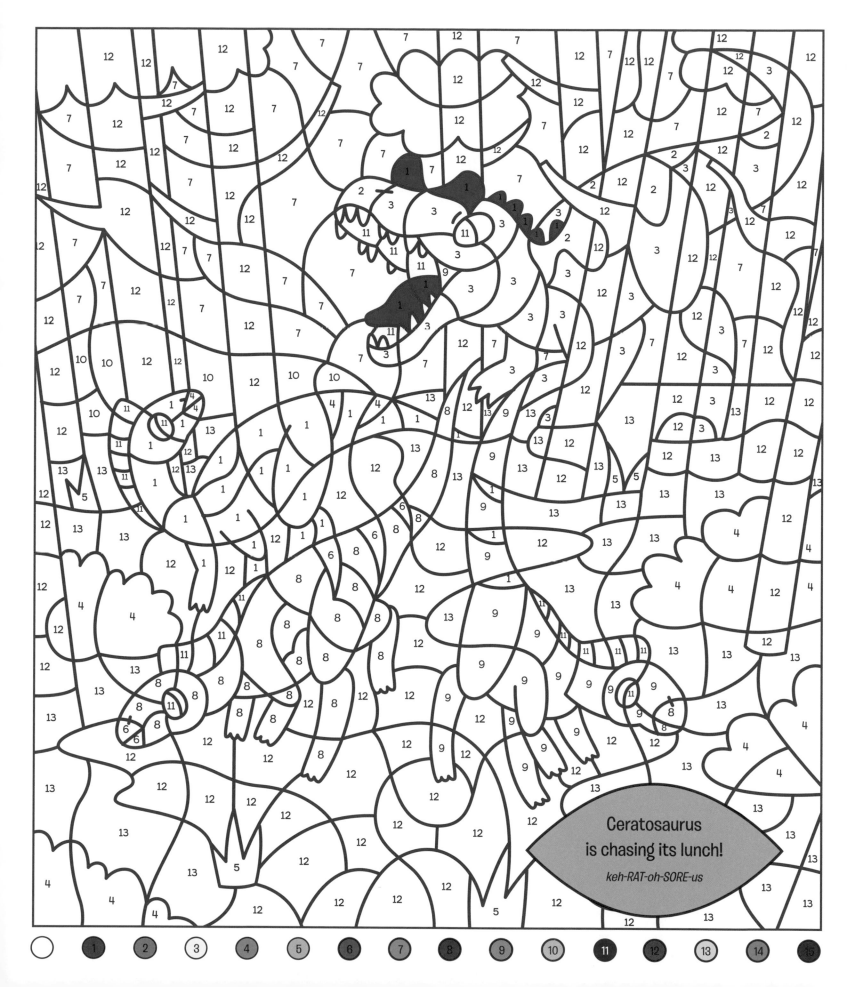

Ceratosaurus is chasing its lunch!

keh-RAT-oh-SORE-us

Up and down,
and round and round.
We all love a merry-go-round!

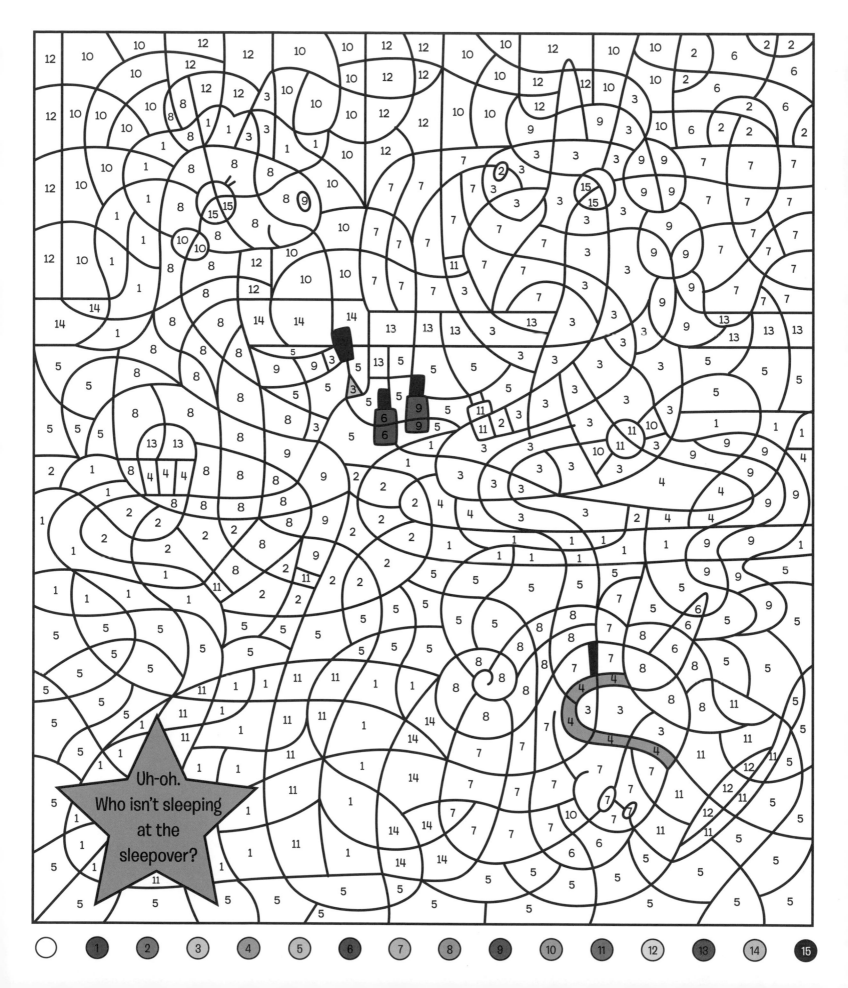

Uh-oh. Who isn't sleeping at the sleepover?

Some goats have very long ears.

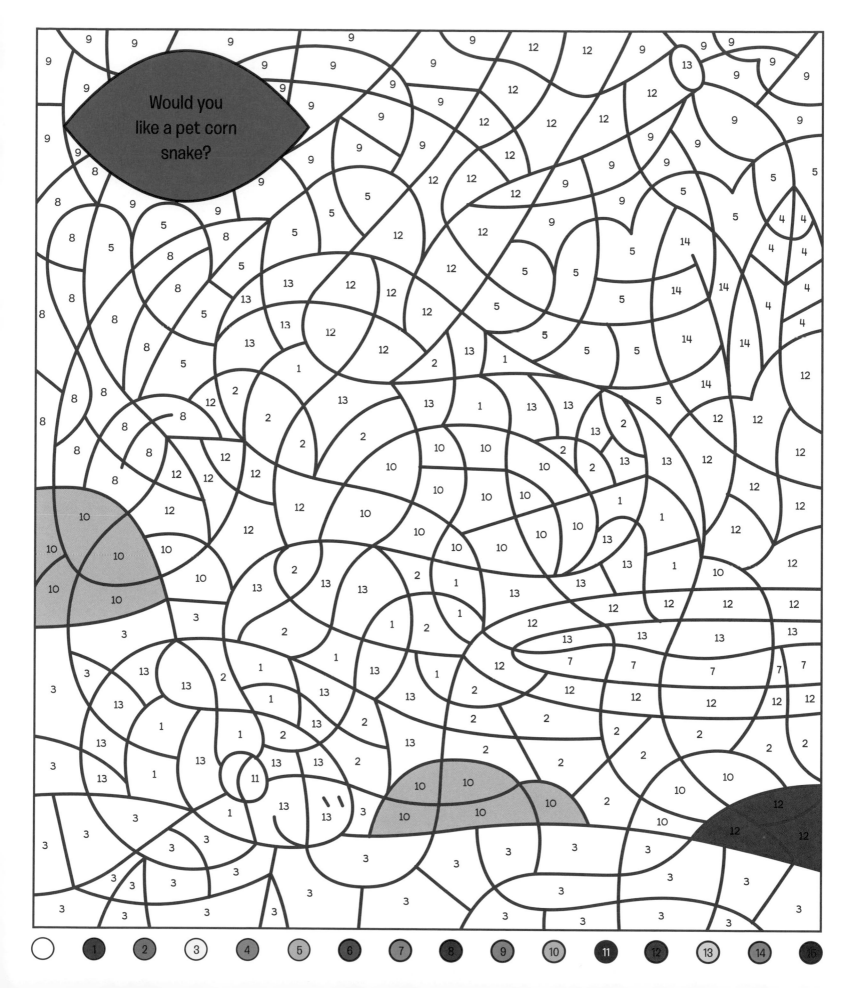

Lambeosaurus sounds the alarm.

LAM-be-uh-SORE-us

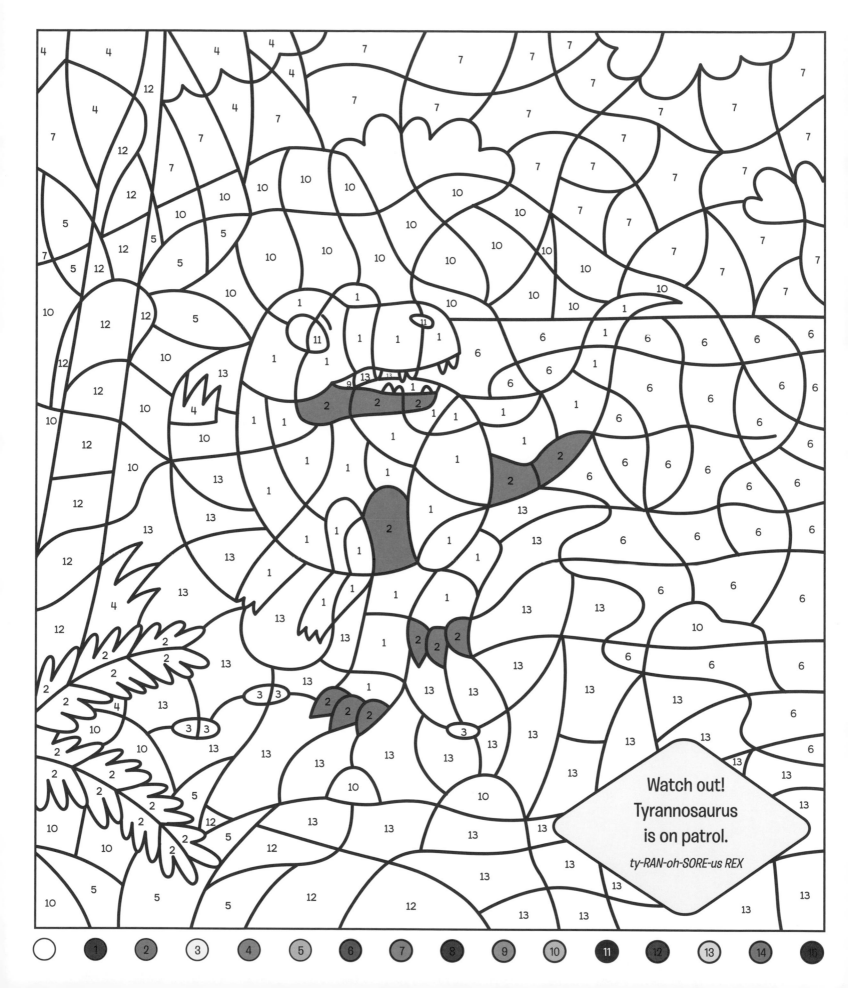

Watch out! Tyrannosaurus is on patrol.

ty-RAN-oh-SORE-us REX

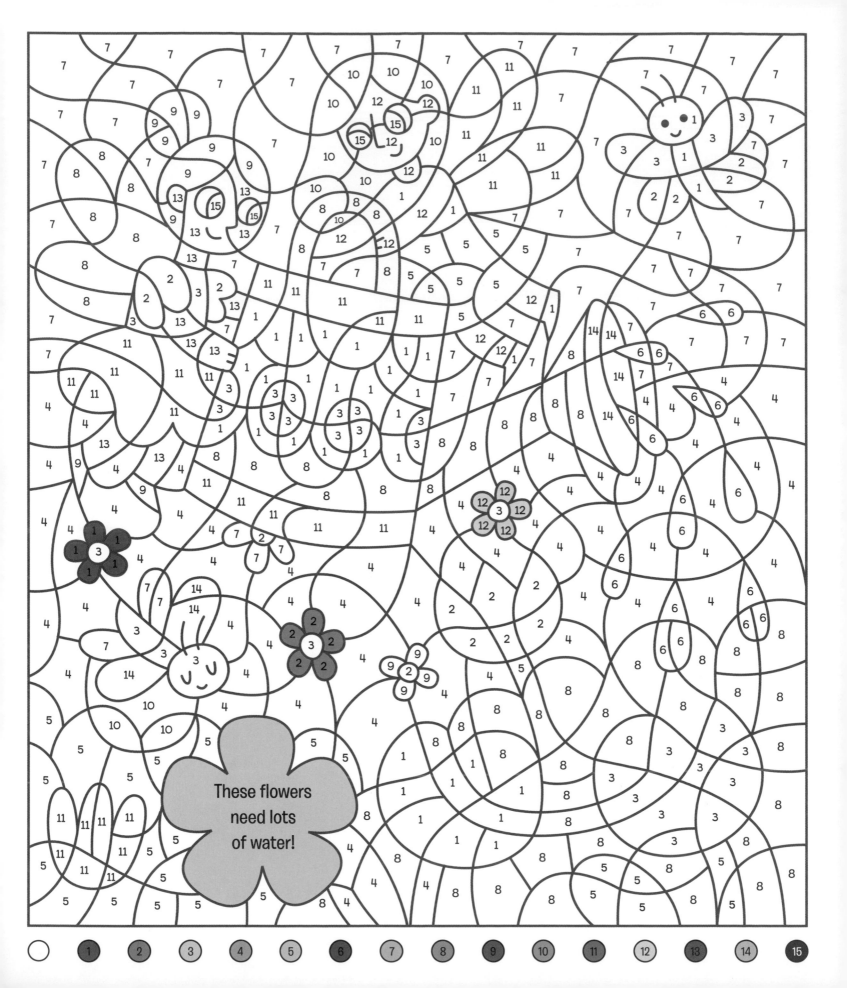

These flowers
need lots
of water!

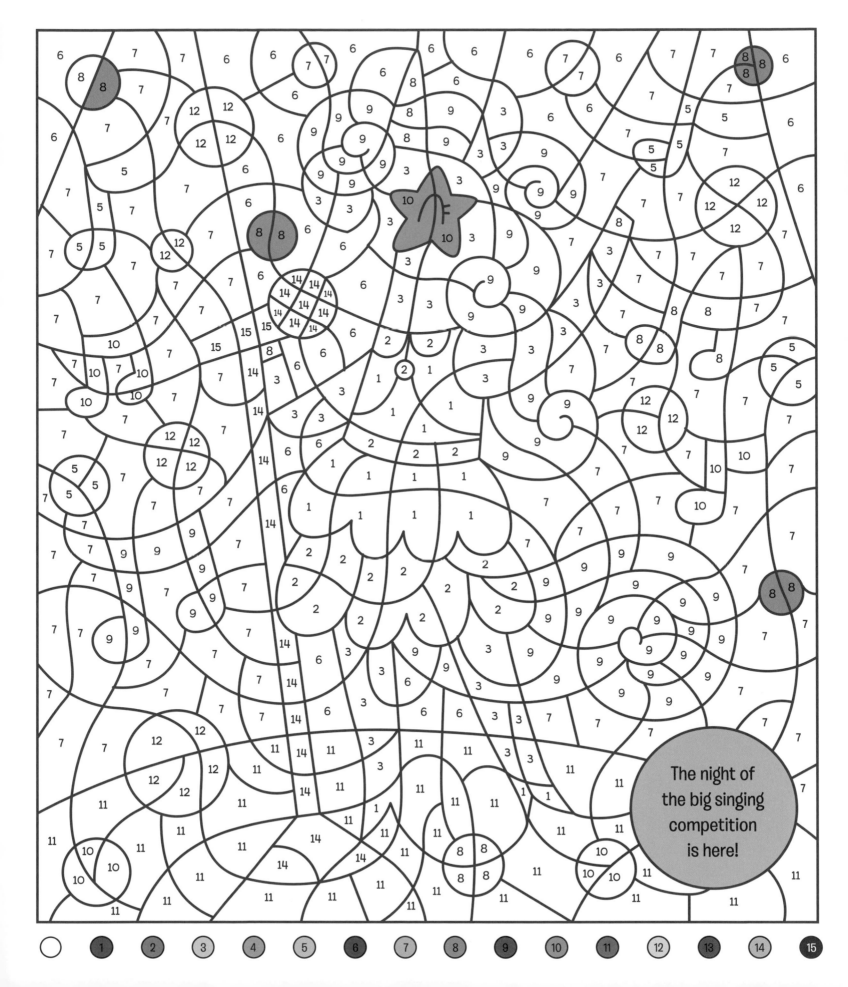

The night of the big singing competition is here!

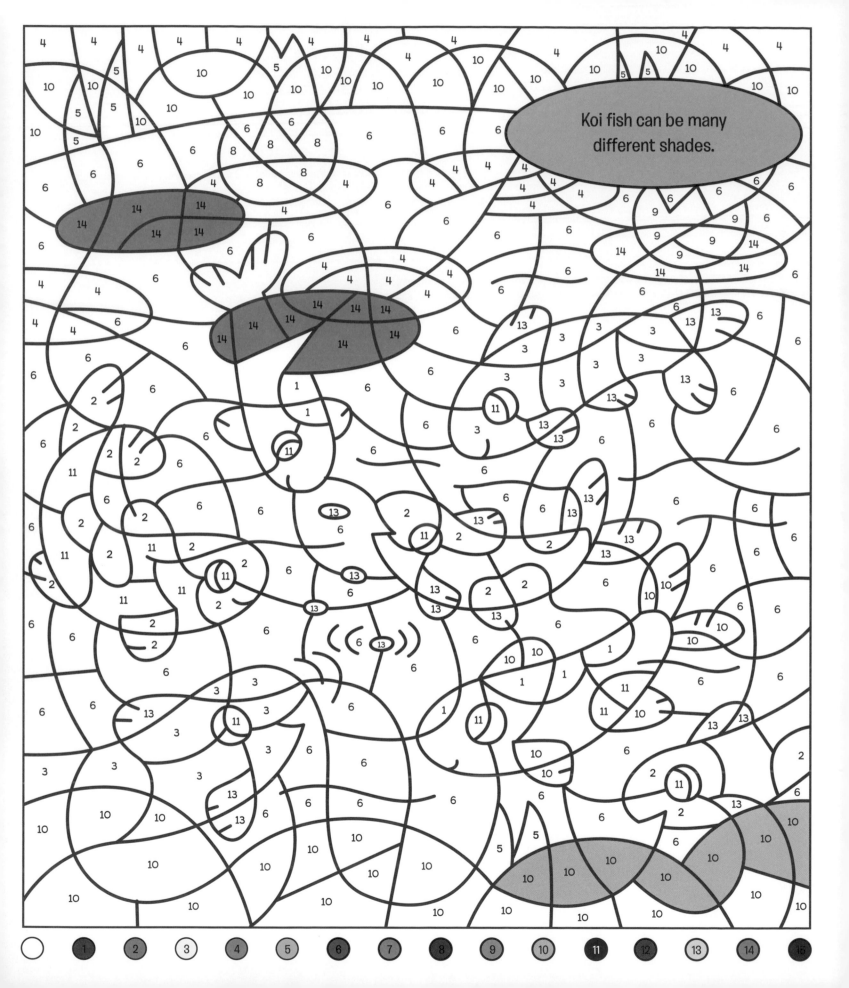

Koi fish can be many different shades.

Let's visit the dog groomer!

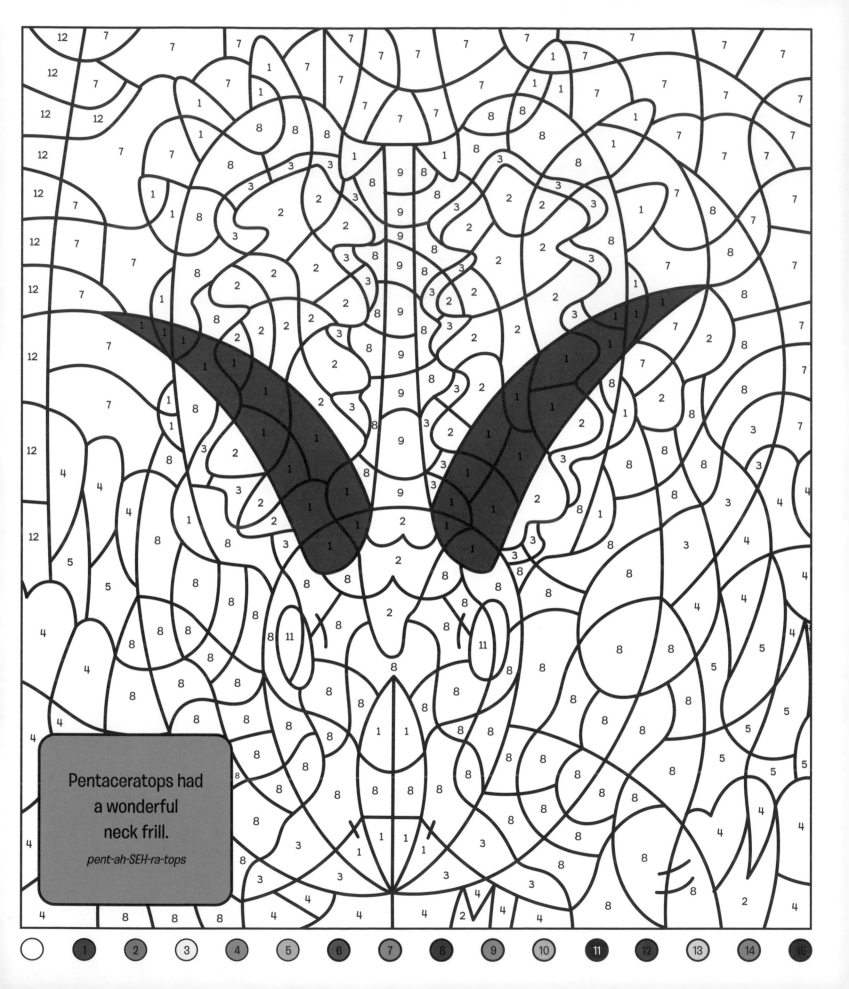

Pentaceratops had a wonderful neck frill.

pent-ah-SEH-ra-tops

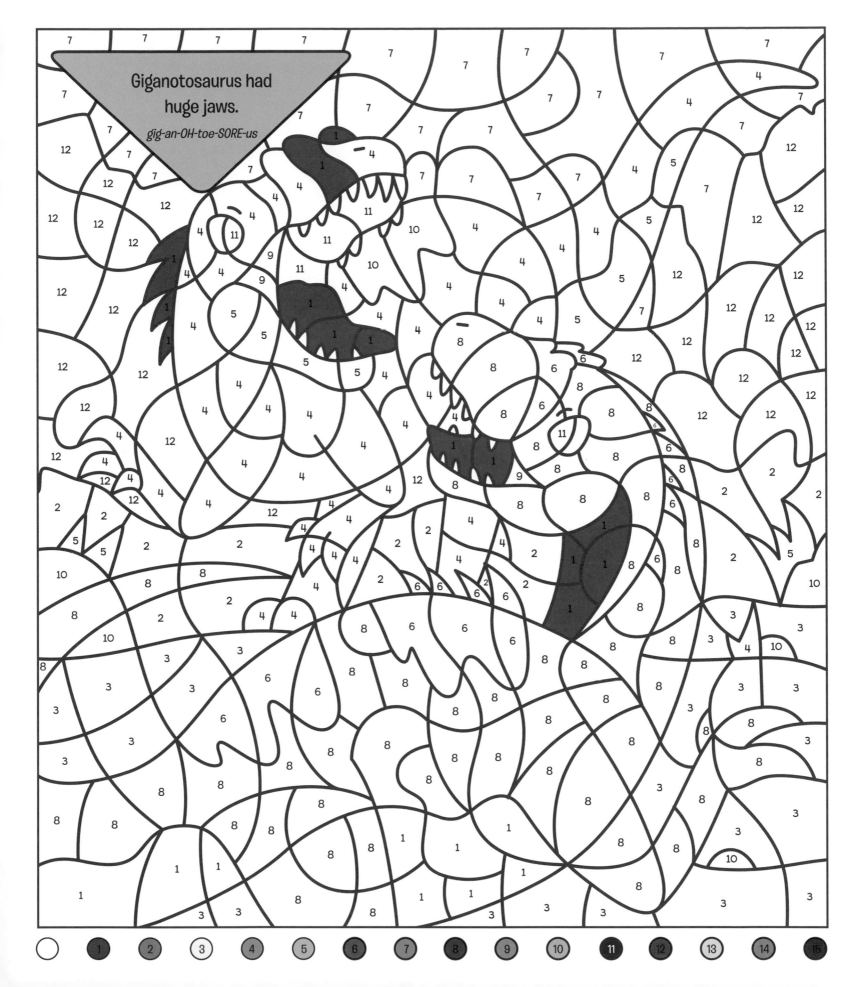

Giganotosaurus had huge jaws.

gig-an-OH-toe-SORE-us

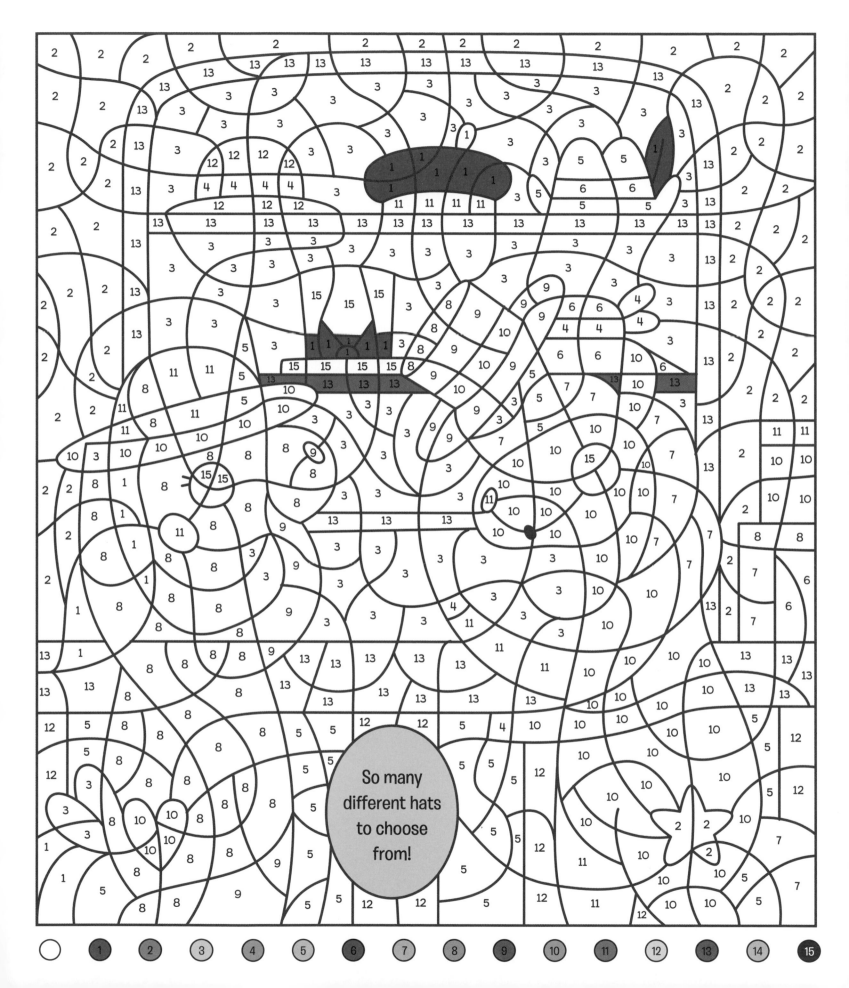

So many different hats to choose from!

Mini pigs
are very
clever.

Cats are good at climbing trees.

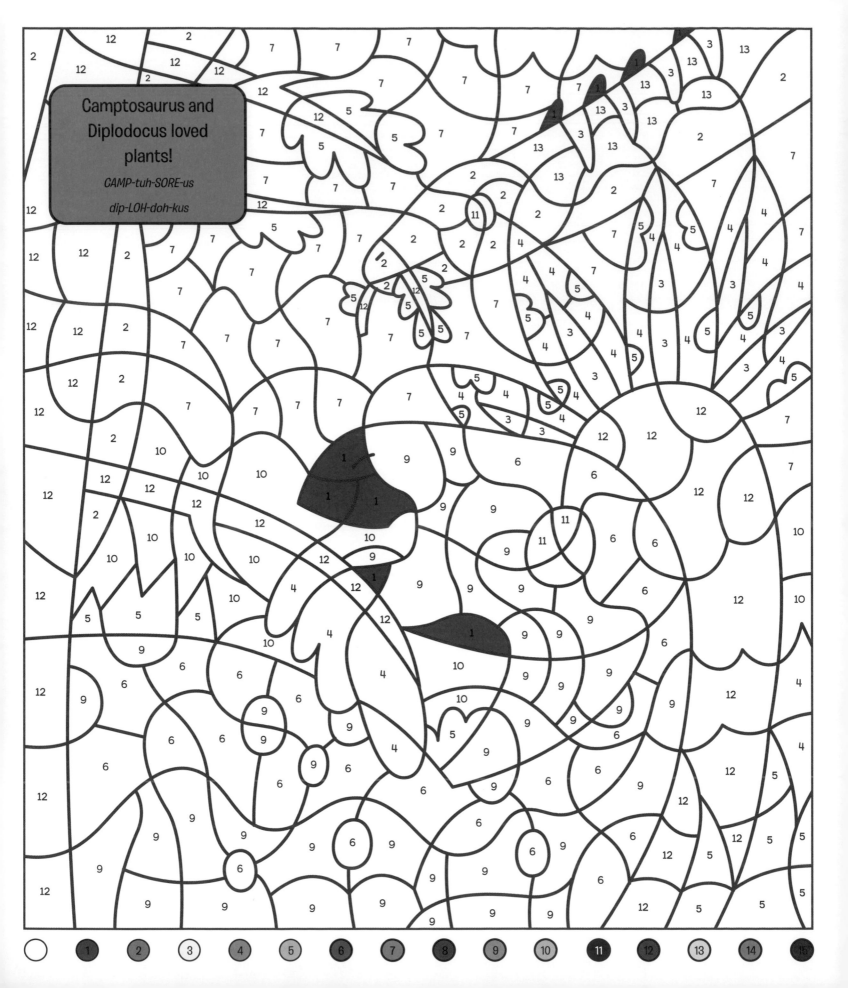

Camptosaurus and Diplodocus loved plants!

CAMP-tuh-SORE-us

dip-LOH-doh-kus

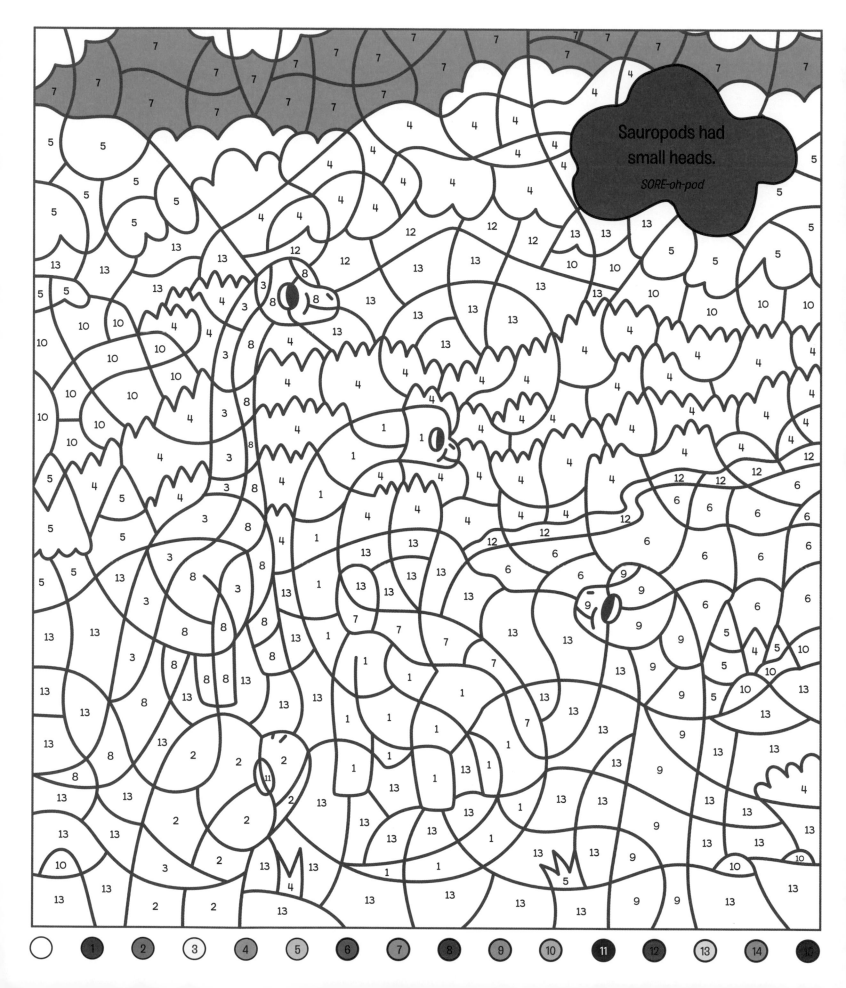

Sauropods had small heads.

SORE-oh-pod

An early yoga class is the best way to start the day!

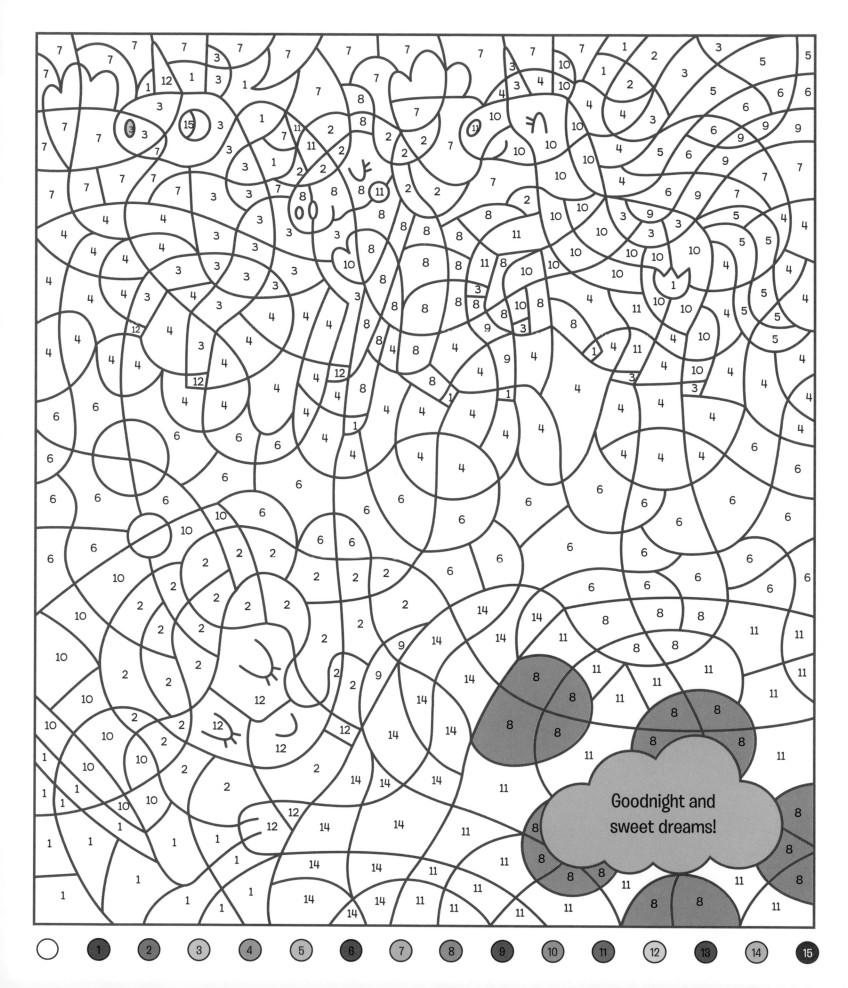

Goodnight and sweet dreams!

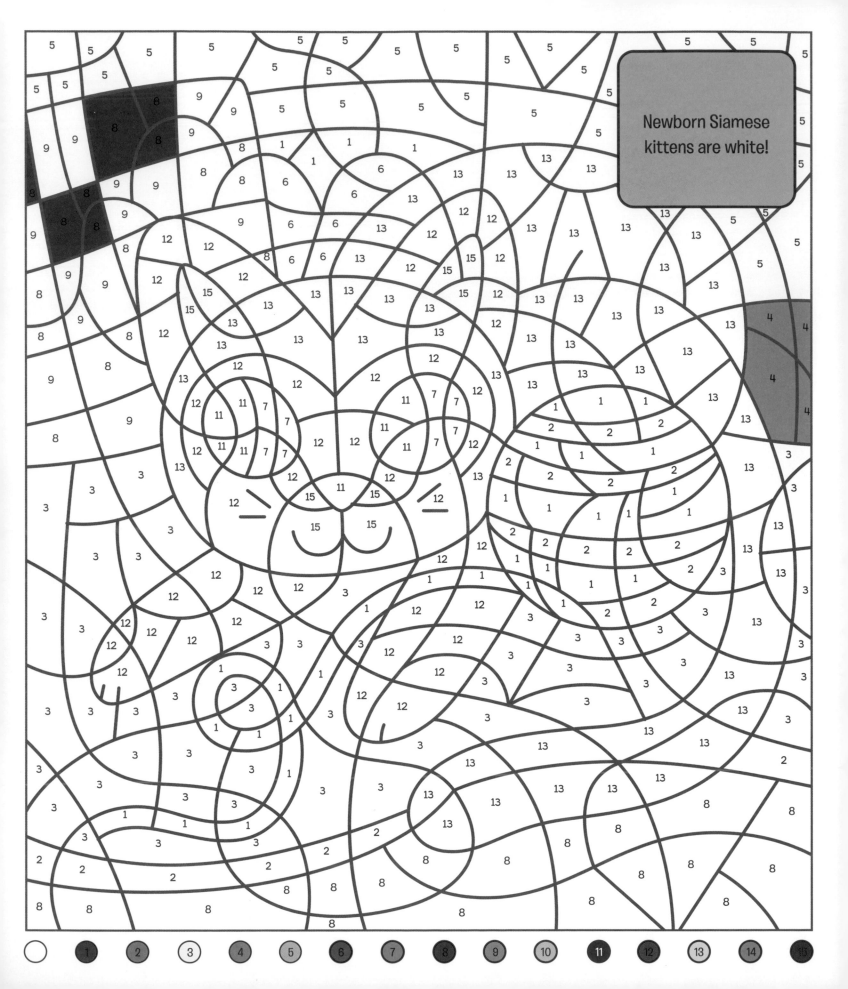

Newborn Siamese kittens are white!

A group of geese is called a "gaggle."

Ornithocheirus had a crest on its beak.

OR-nith-oh-KY-rus

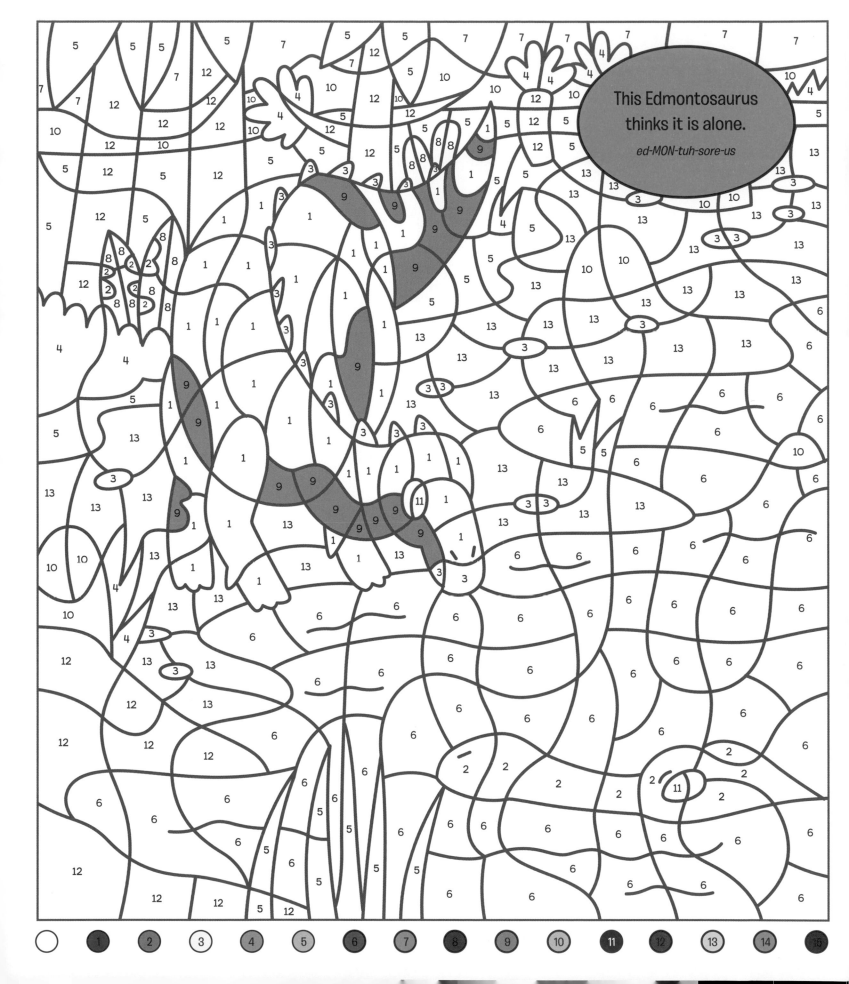

This Edmontosaurus thinks it is alone.

ed-MON-tuh-sore-us

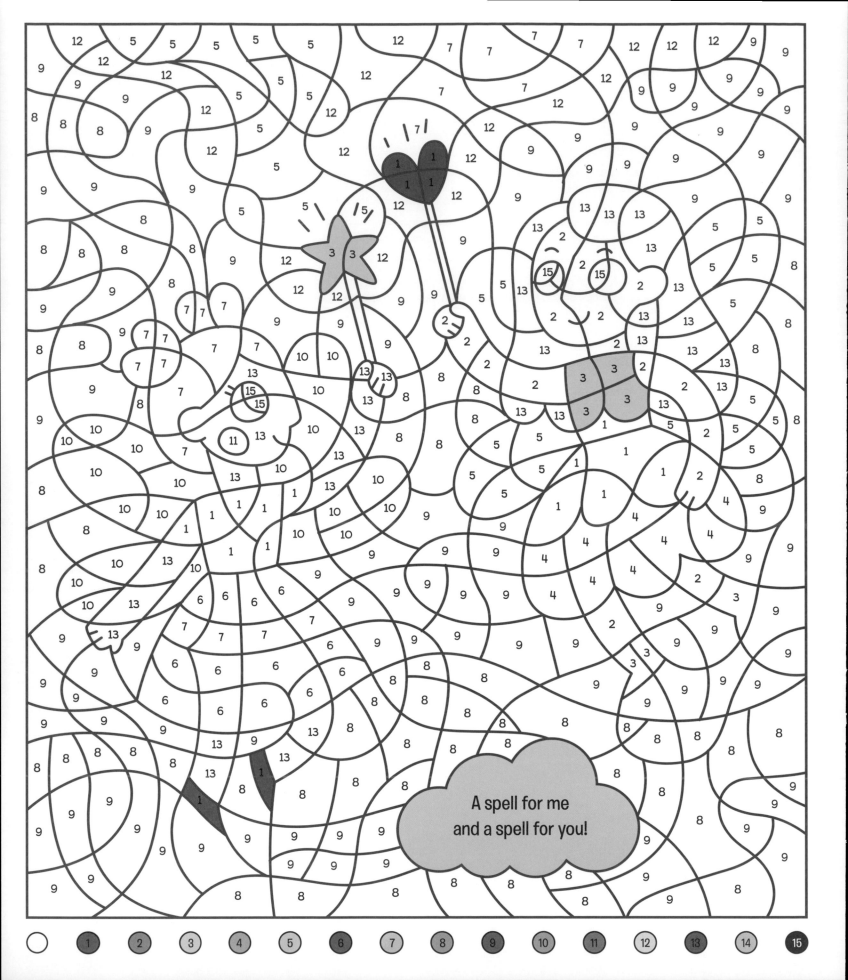

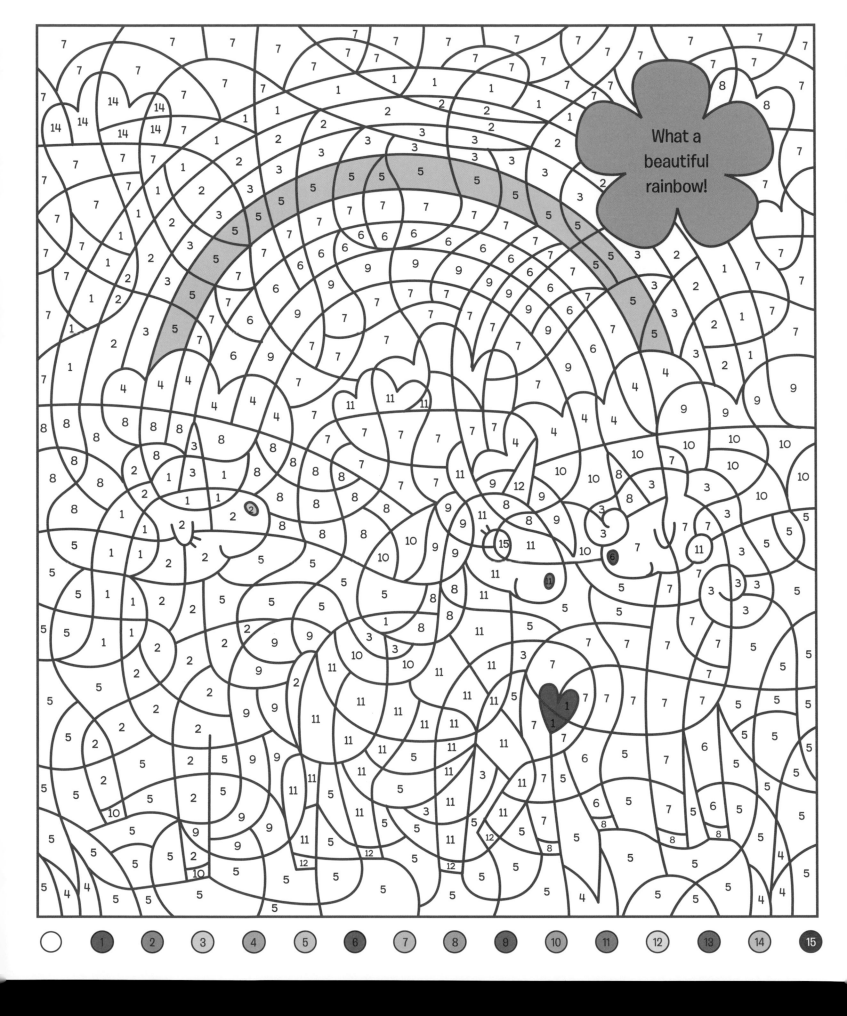

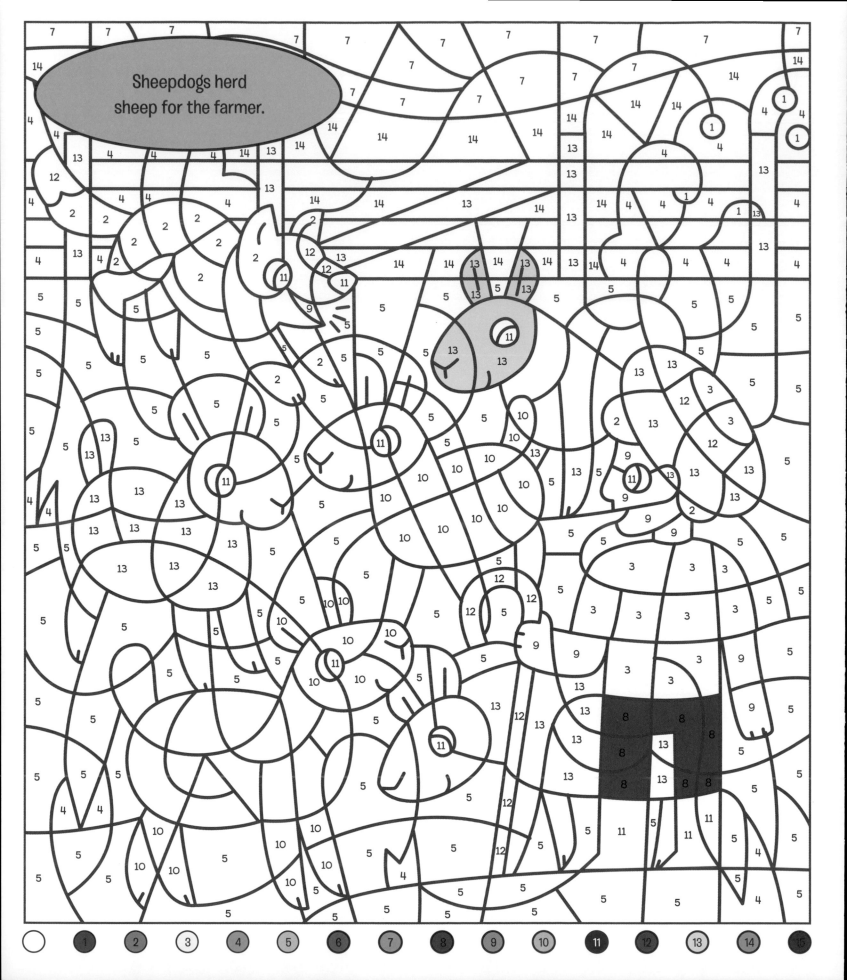

Sheepdogs herd sheep for the farmer.

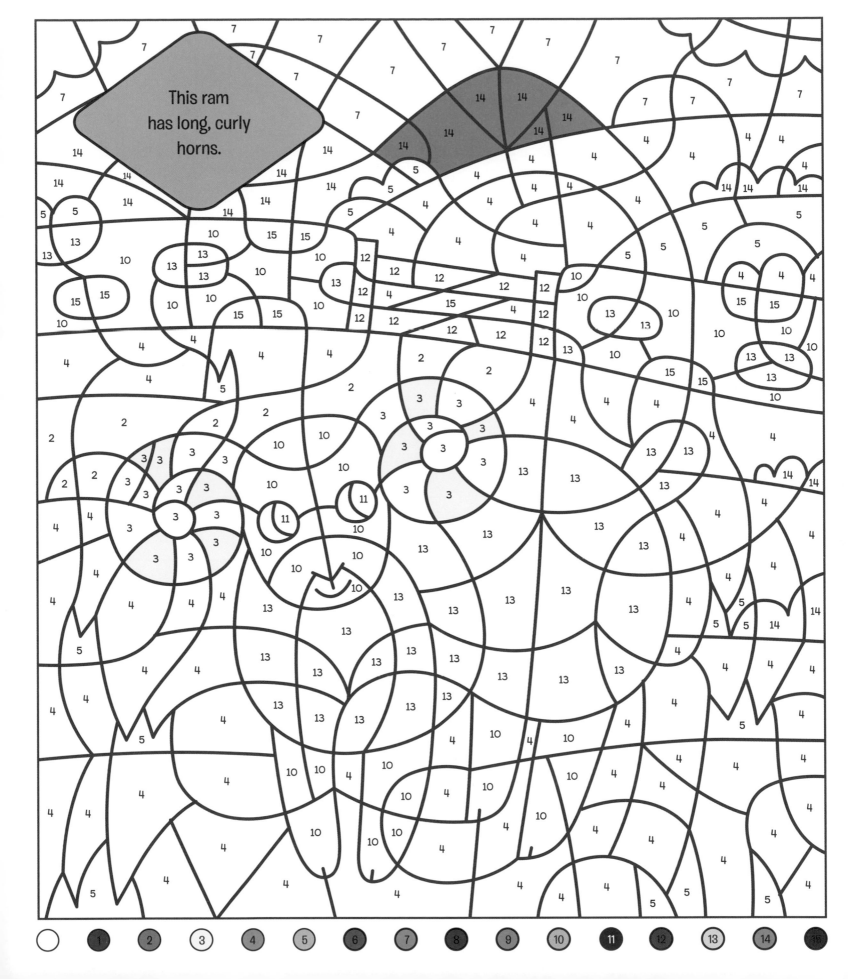

This ram has long, curly horns.

Herds of Titanosauruses moved very slowly!

ty-TAN-oh-SORE-us

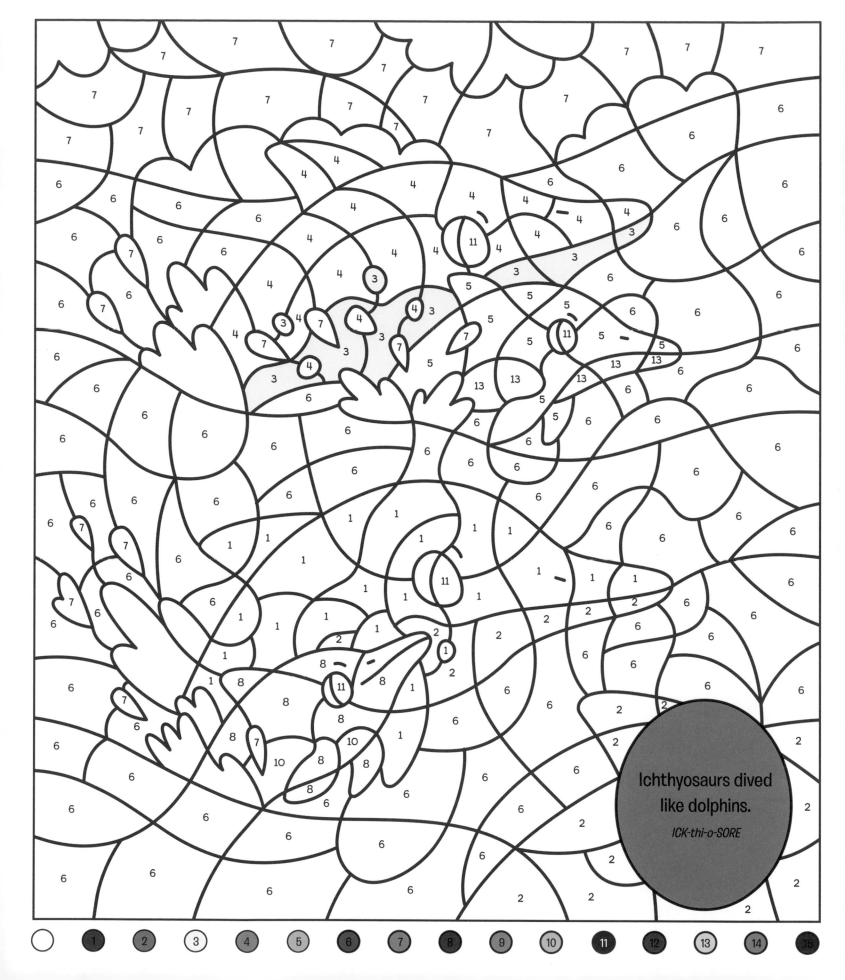

Ichthyosaurs dived like dolphins.

ICK-thi-o-SORE

Blow out the candle and make a wish!

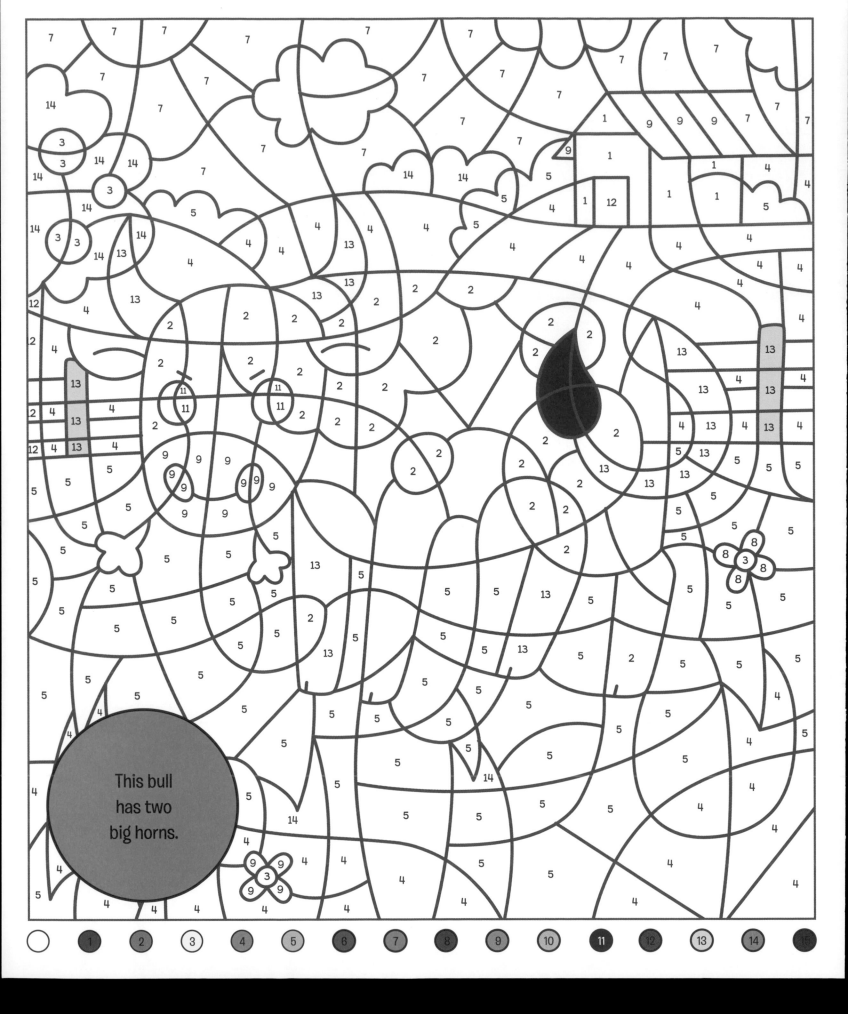

This bull has two big horns.

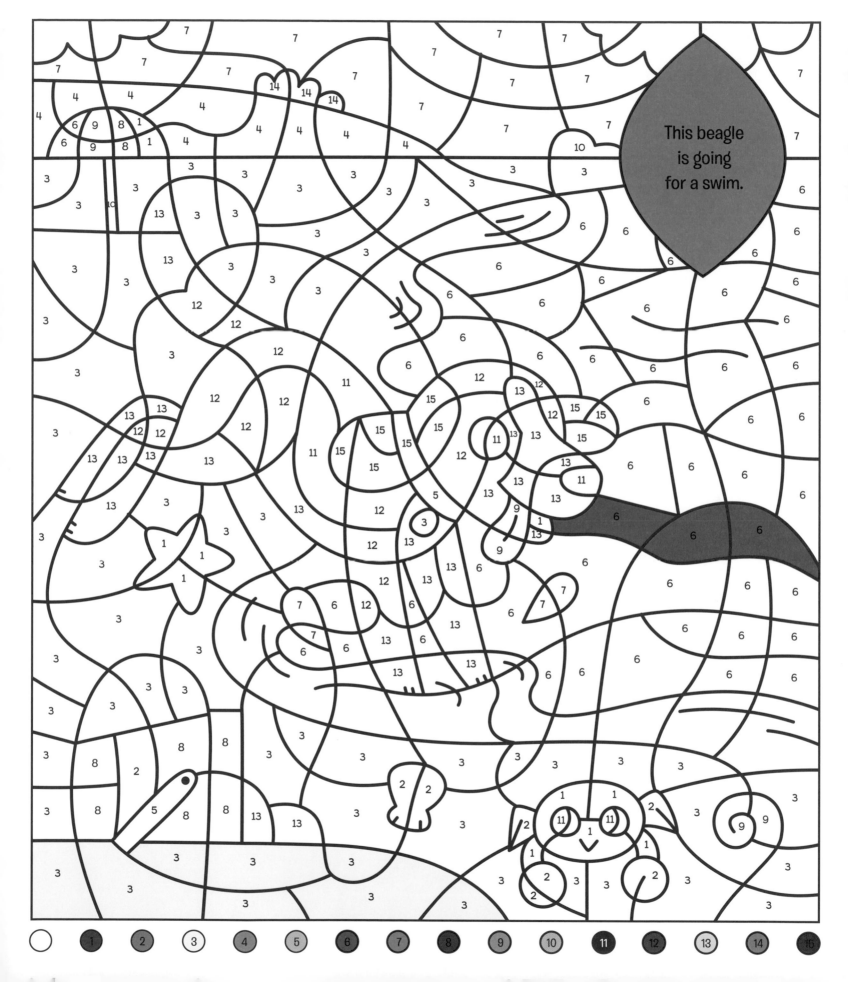

This beagle is going for a swim.

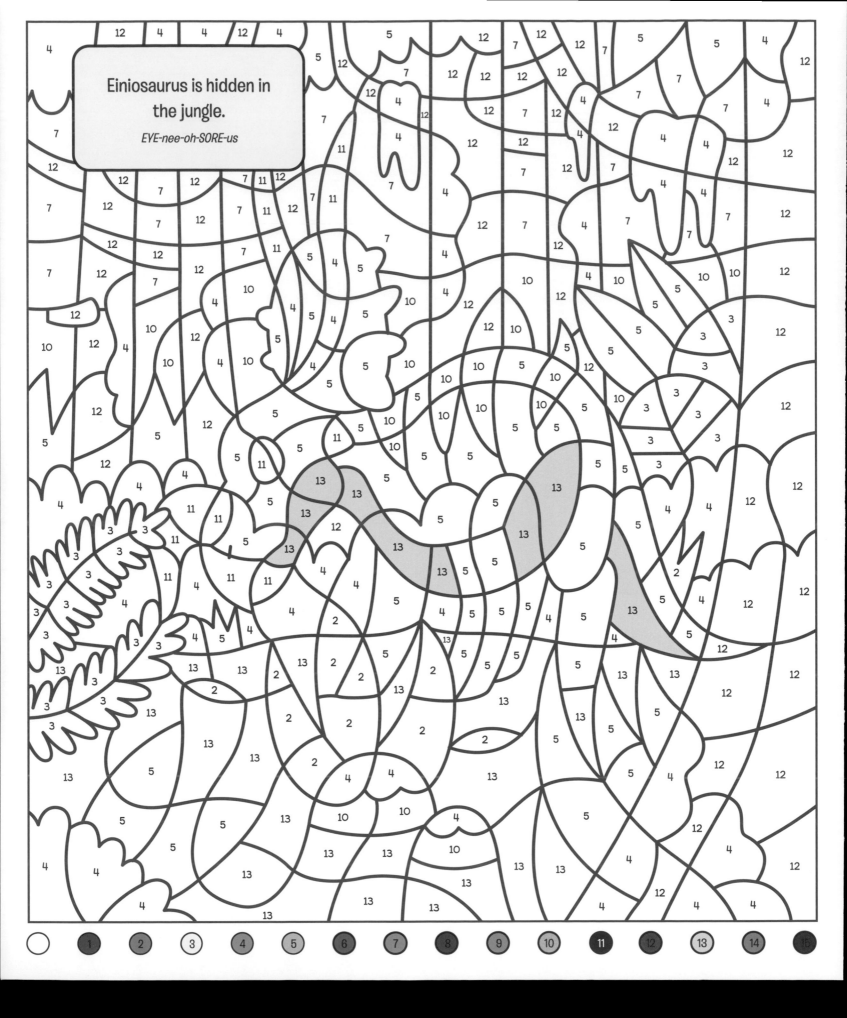

Einiosaurus is hidden in the jungle.

EYE-nee-oh-SORE-us

Gargoyleosaurus
ate ferns.

gar-GOYL-ee-oh-SORE-us

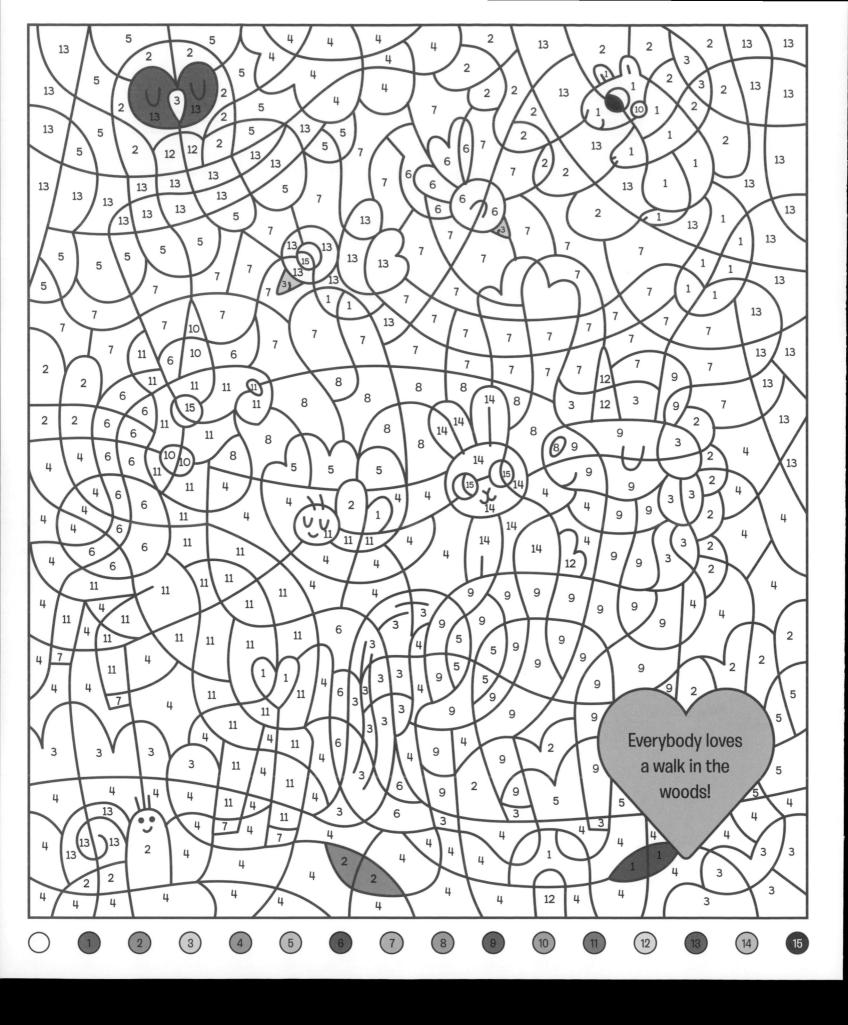

Everybody loves a walk in the woods!

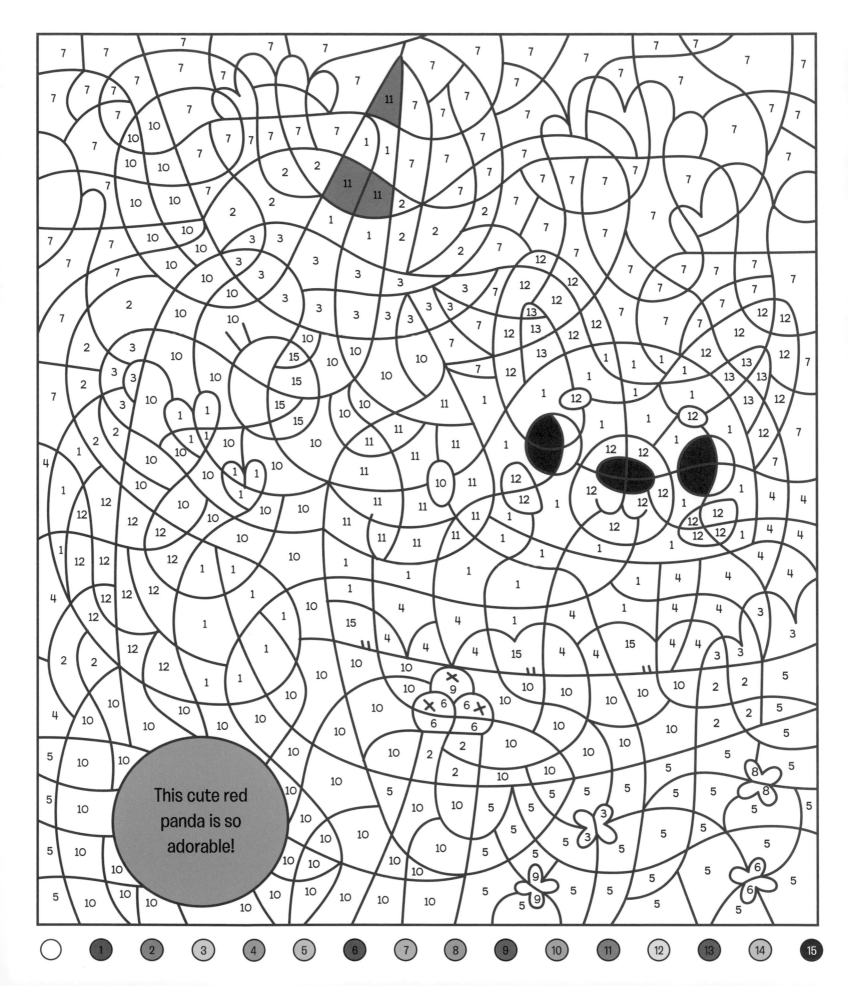

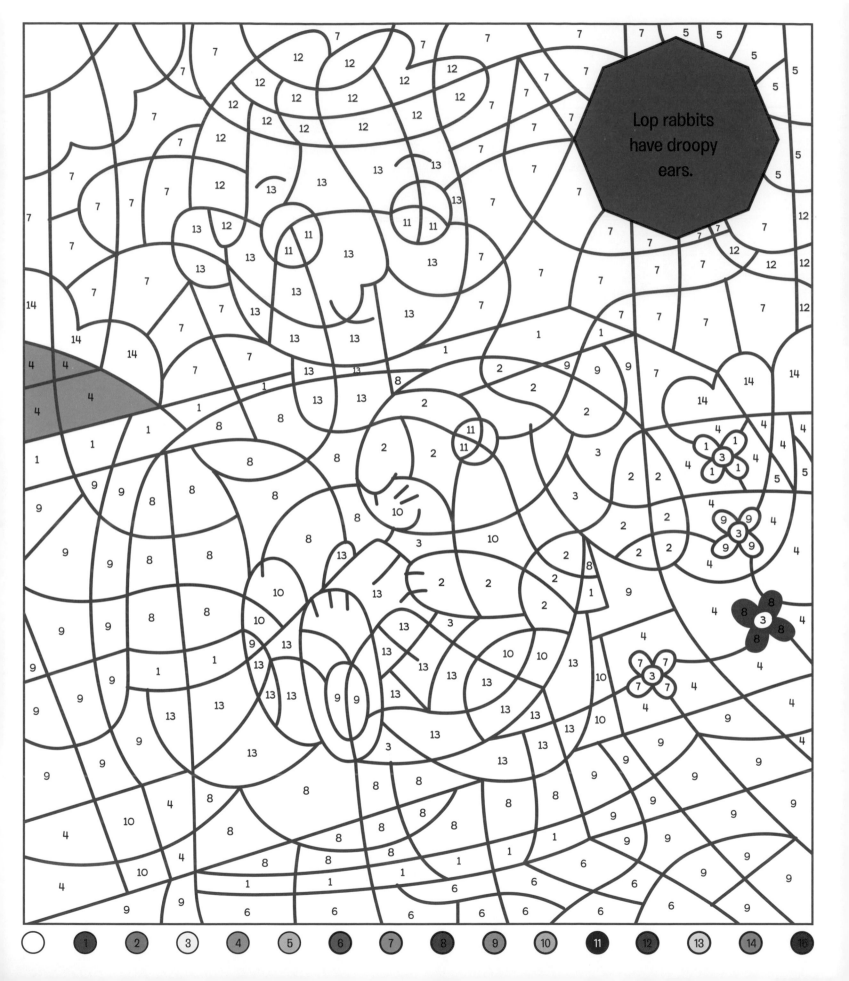

Lop rabbits have droopy ears.

Shetland ponies are very small.

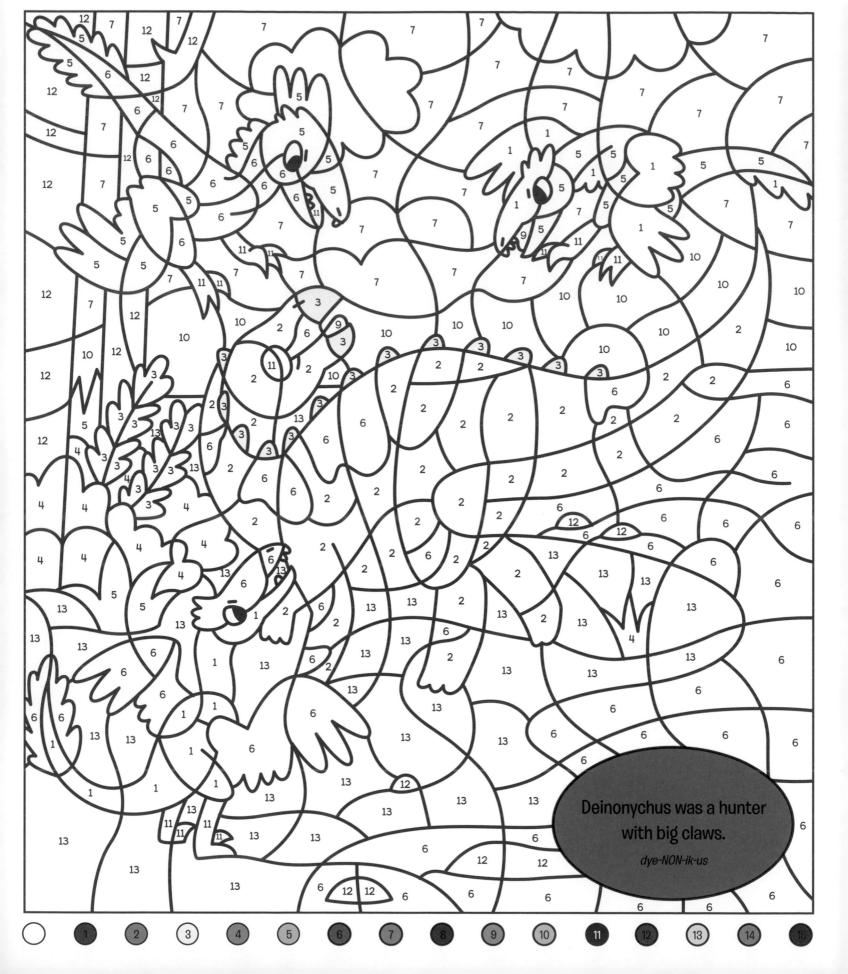

Deinonychus was a hunter with big claws.

dye-NON-ik-us

Parasuchus looked like a crocodile.

PAH-rah-SOO-kus

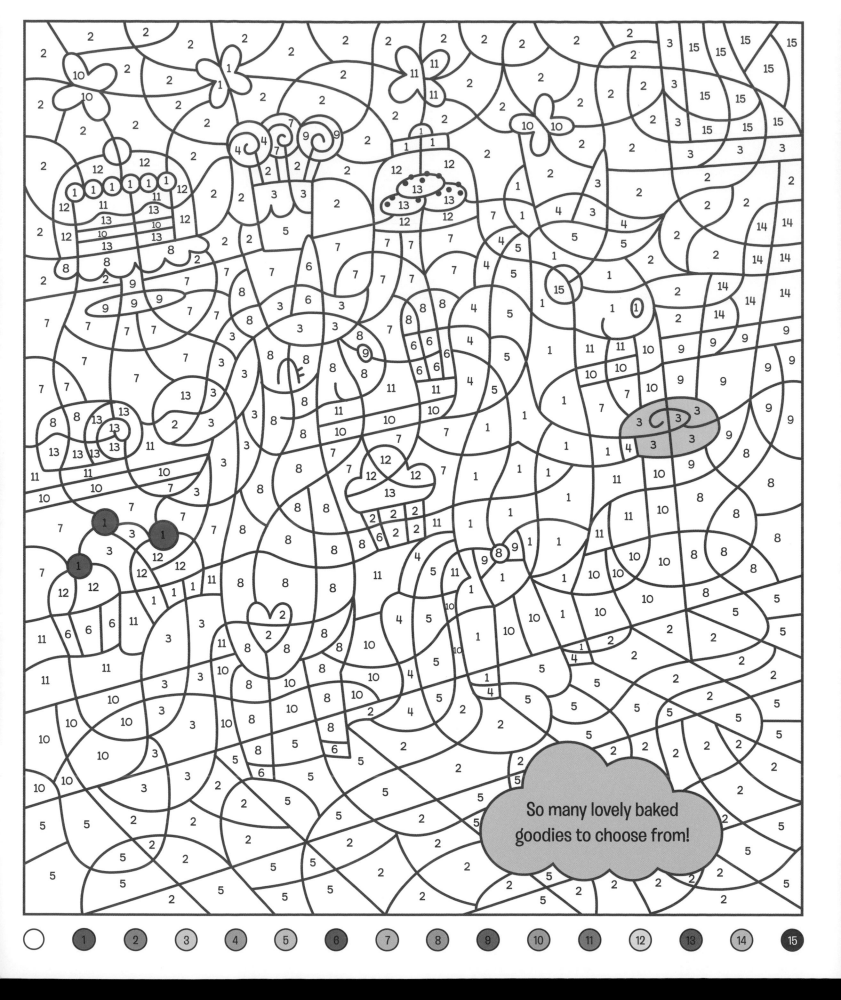

So many lovely baked goodies to choose from!

Who lives in this beautiful fairy-tale castle?

Ducklings feel at home on water.